REVISED EDITION

A WRITER'S BOOK OF DAYS

A Spirited Companion & Lively Muse for the Writing Life

JUDY REEVES

Foreword by **JANET FITCH**

New World Library
Novato, California

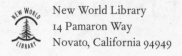

New World Library
14 Pamaron Way
Novato, California 94949

Page 18: Jack Kerouac, "Belief & Technique for Modern Prose — List of Essentials." Reprinted by permission of Sterling Lord Literistic, Inc. © 1977 by Jack Kerouac.

Page 131: Brenda Ueland, "If You Want to Write." Excerpt from chapter XVIII, © 1987 by the Estate of Brenda Ueland. Reprinted from *If You Want to Write: A Book about Art, Independence and Spirit* with the permission of Graywolf Press, Saint Paul, Minnesota.

Page 194: Scott Russell Sanders, "The Most Human Art," is excerpted from "The Power of Stories," which was originally published by the *Georgia Review*. © 1997 by Scott Russell Sanders. Reprinted by permission of the author.

Text design by Megan Colman and Tona Pearce Myers

Library of Congress Cataloging-in-Publication Data
Reeves, Judith, date.
A writer's book of days : a spirited companion & lively muse for the writing life / Judy Reeves ; foreword by Janet Fitch. — Rev. ed.
    p. cm.
Includes bibliographical references.
ISBN 978-1-57731-936-8 (pbk. : alk. paper)
1. Authorship—Miscellanea. 2. Creative writing—Miscellanea. I. Title.
PN165.R44 2010
808'.02—dc22   2010020702

First printing of revised edition, September 2010
ISBN 978-1-57731-936-8
Printed in Canada on 100% postconsumer-waste recycled paper

 New World Library is a proud member of the Green Press Initiative.

10 9 8 7 6 5 4 3 2 1

PRAISE FOR *A WRITER'S BOOK OF DAYS*

"As a teacher, I have shamelessly stolen writing prompts from this wonderful book for years. As a writer, I have done some of my very best writing as a result of them. I am absolutely thrilled by this newest incarnation and can't wait to both share it with my students and use it for my own work. It will always hold a spot next to such classics as *Writing Down the Bones* and *Bird by Bird* on my bookshelf."

— Tammy Greenwood, author of *Two Rivers*

"A delightful mix of common sense and inspiration, *A Writer's Book of Days* provides the voice of the teacher, coach, friend, and support group available on call. I suggest this book to every writing seminar graduate — a way to take the experience home and carry on."

— Christina Baldwin, author of *Storycatcher*, *The Seven Whispers*, *Life's Companion*, and *The Circle Way*

"Because of Judy Reeves's extraordinary encouragement, embodied in her newly revised classic, *A Writer's Book of Days*, our profession today is blessed by authors who are more imaginative, more savvy, and more assiduous than they would have been had Judy not given so much of her intuition and talent to our community and our craft. May she evermore inspire us to search for and find ourselves in our writing."

— Thomas Larson, author of *The Saddest Music Ever Written: The Story of Samuel Barber's* Adagio for Strings

"*A Writer's Book of Days* is an invaluable guide for the writer who's blocked or stuck or simply unable to get the writing done. Full of delicious prompts, exercises, insights, and inspirational tips, it will get people who dream of becoming real writers to do what real writers do — sit down joyfully and get to work!"

— Steve Kowit, author of *In the Palm of Your Hand: The Poet's Portable Workshop*

"*A Writer's Book of Days* is the best sort of writer's book: You feel like writing as you read it! It is a spring-fed fountain of inspiration for the writers in us all. This book dances around the imagination and makes you take out your pens and notebook to play."

— SARK, artist/author of *Succulent Wild Woman* and *Glad No Matter What*

"Reeves is a cheerleader. . . . Many writers have the best intentions upon sitting down, but feel they lack something to write about. Reeves directs that desire to write by offering daily topics and then encouraging the writer to take them wherever their own personal response leads. Just write!"
— *BookPage*

"How I wish I'd had this book forty years ago when I decided to become a writer! Reeves not only provides the creative inspiration to get us writing and keep us going, she suggests exactly the right themes and daily writings to tease out the spiritual gifts of our own creative voices. If you love writing, you've got to have this book in your library."
— Hal Zina Bennett, author of *Write Starts*, *Write from the Heart*, and many other books of nonfiction and fiction

"Hats off to Judy Reeves for this practical compendium for the budding writer. Writers have long known that daily practice is what it takes, and Reeves gives us a helping hand with daily writing exercises, useful inspirations, and pertinent quotes by sources ranging from Mick Jagger to Willa Cather. This Book of Days is not for the shelf but for the backpack, the desk, the bedside table. A portable feast."
— Dorianne Laux, professor of creative writing, University of Oregon, and coauthor of *The Poet's Companion: A Guide to the Pleasures of Writing Poetry*

"How marvelous when a creative stream pours through the psyche and we are there to write the words! Judy Reeves knows how fragile these moments are, how susceptible to our lack of courage, to enticements, to chores. *A Writer's Book of Days* counters those evils with a detailed practice: an exercise, encouraging suggestions, and quotes from working writers on nearly every page. Fine help for developing those precious moments when the words do flow."
— Clive Matson, poet, author of *Let the Crazy Child Write!*

A Writer's
Book of Days

Also by Judy Reeves

A Creative Writer's Kit:
A Spirited Companion & Lively Muse for the Writing Life

The Writer's Retreat Kit:
A Guide for Creative Exploration & Personal Expression

Writing Alone, Writing Together:
A Guide for Writers and Writing Groups

To all the
Brown Baggers, Thursday Writers, and Marathoners
who have put pen to page

The writer, perhaps more than any of his fellow artists, has access to the human subconscious. His words sink deep, shaping dreams, easing the pain of loneliness, banishing incantations and omens, keeping alive the memories of the race, providing intimations of immortality, nourishing great anticipations, sharpening the instinct for justice, and imparting respect for the fragility of life. These functions are essential for human evolution.

— NORMAN COUSINS

CONTENTS

MARCH

APRIL

MAY

JUNE

JULY

AUGUST

SEPTEMBER

OCTOBER

NOVEMBER

DECEMBER

FOREWORD

Like all writers, I have a secret stash of writing books, a kind of life vest for when I'm drowning in my own insipidity, a prybar for my own creativity when it seems hopelessly jammed and I'm left scratching at the lid, breaking my nails off. My stash lives on a shelf just behind my desk, where I can browse for a few minutes when I feel so stale I can't even imagine writing anything of value.

A Writer's Book of Days has resided on that shelf since 1999.

I met Judy Reeves in the mid '90s, when she was running The Writing Center in San Diego. She gave me one of my very first teaching jobs. A master teacher in her own right, Reeves regularly taught classes at standing-room capacity. But she was best known for her "brown bag workshops" — lunchtime writing groups that incorporated freewriting prompts, easily accessible to new writers, equally useful for pros. These lunchtime sprints helped writers remember their jobs were simply that — jobs. That *writing* was what they really *did*.

Reeves has never stopped inspiring writers, from the greenest tyro to the most masterful auteur. You can never be too well read or too inspired. (Who cares about thin and rich!) Our skill levels may differ, beginner or expert, but the process is the same — you're always trying to pull the rabbit out of that darn hat.

Since *A Writer's Book of Days* first appeared, I have recommended it to literally hundreds of writers. Any time someone asks me for writing tips —

How can I start? What do you do about writer's block? — I suggest they peruse this wonderful compendium of writing lore, empathy, and daily practice, including the kind of writing prompts which have pulled many a struggling author out of the corner of his or her own imaginative cul-de-sac.

And personally, I'm excited at the appearance of this revised edition, and a year's worth of new prompts! For me, those small doorways — *"Write about a time you got what you wanted" "Write about falling"* — have always supplied the book's most valuable function. When I feel I've used up every inch of my creativity and knowledge about the world, prompts such as these help me get back into the unconscious place where the rabbit still lives, waiting to be grabbed by its furry ruff and pulled from the hat yet again.

I wish you good writing!

— Janet Fitch
Author of *Paint It Black* and *White Oleander*

INTRODUCTION

When I wrote the introduction to the first edition of this book in March 1999, I had just returned from a regular session of the Brown Bag Group, a writing practice group that had been meeting weekly for more than five years. Tomorrow I'll participate in another session of the Brown Baggers, eleven years later and nearly seventeen years since the group first began.

Amazingly, some of the same writers who've been participating since the early days will meet around the same tables, hand painted with brilliant fish swimming in an azure sea. We'll be joined by six or eight or ten others — writers with day jobs who come on their lunch hour, self-employed writers who call their own hours, writers whose day jobs are at night, writers who've been laid off their jobs, and writers whose full-time job is writing. All of us come together to spend fifteen or seventeen minutes hunched over our notebooks, writing in response to a prompt that's pulled from a cigar box, then reading aloud what we've written. We meet in a different location than we used to, and the prompts change every session, but virtually everything else is the same as it was more than a decade ago.

That's not to say our writing hasn't changed. For most of us, it has. Regular writing practice with the group and alone has made a difference in the way we write. We come to the page a little more easily, with fewer expectations, maybe a bit less anxiety. We're softer with ourselves, which has made our writing stronger, more authentic. Some of us have found our voices and the genre that best suits what we have to say, and from our practice pages have evolved stories, novels, memoirs, and more, many of them published. Others are just beginning the journey, brave travelers whose only compass is their pen and their single map, a blank page. Stick around, we say. Expect surprises.

After all these years of writing alone and with groups, I am still delighted by the surprises that come from the freewheeling, free-falling intensity of timed, focused writing to a prompt. I never know from one session to the next what will show up — fragments of a long-ago memory, the stub of a story with characters I've never seen before, a rewriting of yesterday's therapy session, or, blessing of blessings, a poem.

When I first set out on this journey, I was a woman who, since third grade, wanted nothing more than to "be a writer." But in actual truth, I hadn't written much at all aside from the journals and diaries I'd kept off and on since adolescence. Now, looking behind me after nearly twenty years of regular writing practice, I see a trail marked with box after heavy box of worn and shaggy notebooks. The better part of two novels, stories, bits and pieces of memoir and personal narrative, explorations and false starts — some of it just plain junk. But it's my junk, and even the junk is testimony to time put in doing the thing I believe I was meant to do: writing.

If you feel the same, this book might be for you.

In my classes, I sometimes ask students to write about their experiences with writing and themselves as writers. The stories I hear are similar: "I always wanted to be a writer. I started writing when I was young. Poems and little stories. But I could never finish anything. I'd put it all away and wouldn't write for a while. But then something would make me want to start again. So I'd write more poems and stories. I even started a novel once. But I'd get busy doing something else and drift away from it. Now I feel like something is missing from my life. And I want to write again."

These students and others, whose stories differ only in some of the details, have one thing in common: even though their spirits long for it, they have never made writing a priority in their lives; that is, they have never set aside a specific time for their writing. They don't practice the craft.

My grandmother used to tell me that when we're born God puts His big thumbprint in the middle of our forehead and says, "You're a musician,"

"You're a baker," "You make pottery," and so on. To some of us, He says, "You, you're a writer." Those of us who were marked as writers (or as musicians or painters or dancers) but have pushed aside the calling of the Muse might as well surrender and do the thing we're meant to do. Otherwise, that longing inside our hearts will never be stilled.

This book originally came about because I saw the difference that ongoing, regular writing practice could make in a person's life. I saw it in the lives of my students and those I wrote with in writing practice groups, and I experienced it for myself. A decade later, I am convinced that by integrating regular writing practice sessions into your days, that longing can be stilled. Not only will you fill notebook after notebook; your writing will improve, and so will the quality of your life. Even if you continue to need a day job — and most of us do — your spirit will be gladdened.

There are changes in this revised edition. For one thing, I replaced the term *floppy disk* with *flash drive* and noted the ways computers and the Internet have changed the way we live and the way we write (though I still recommend handwriting with pen and paper for writing practice sessions). I have included more notes on the craft of writing plus new tips and new quotes by writers. There is still a prompt for every day of the year — but these are all new prompts, most of them test-driven by me or other writing practitioners. These new prompts, just like the 365 that preceded them, are guaranteed to work if you give yourself over to them, trust the process, and follow your pen.

May the Muse join you on your journey, and may your writing and your life continue to surprise you.

HOW TO USE THIS BOOK

A stranger to New York City, looking for directions, asks a man on the street, "How do I get to Carnegie Hall?"

"Practice, man," comes the response.

It's an old joke, but the truth is there. In order to get good at anything, you've got to practice. So when somebody asks me, How do I write a novel? Or a short story? An essay, poem, or book? I give them the same answer that man on the street gave: Practice. Practice. Practice.

This idea of writing practice is a new concept to many who want to write. Sure, everybody knows pianists have to train. So do dancers, actors, singers, and athletes. Even artists have sketchbooks, which serve as their practice pages. But there seems to be some vague notion that somewhere deep inside the desire to be a writer is the inherent knowledge of how to go about it. As many a bloody-fingered would-be writer, hip deep in wadded-up paper and frustration, can attest, this just ain't so.

> *Nulla dies sine linea.* Never a day without a line.
>
> ⁀ HORACE ⁀

Natural talent and all the breaks in the world notwithstanding, to become good at anything you've got to do the drills. Lots of drills. To quote Mick Jagger, "You have to sing every day so you can build up to being, you know, amazingly brilliant."

1

WHAT IS WRITING PRACTICE?

Writing practice is showing up at the page. It's running the scales, executing the movements. It's writing for the experience of it, forming the words, capturing the images, filling the pages. Like an artist's sketchbook, a writer's notebook is filled with perspectives, character sketches, shadings, and tones. A writing workout is trying out phrases and auditioning words, letting the imagination have free rein while the editor in your head takes a coffee break. One of the best things about writing practice is that it is practice. It's not supposed to be perfect. You're free to make mistakes, fool around, take risks.

When you show up at the page and put in the time day after day, you learn to trust your pen and the voice that emerges as your own. You name yourself *Writer*.

> I write as a way of exploring something electric.
>
> ⌐ CARY HOLLADAY ⌐

This is what happens: By taking the time for writing practice, you are honoring yourself as writer. When you write on a daily basis, your self-confidence increases. You learn what you want to write about and what matters to you as a writer. You explore your creative nooks and crannies, and foray into some scary places that make your hand tremble and your heart beat faster. This is good. This is when you know you are writing your truth, and that's the best writing anybody ever does. In writing practice, you poke around in your psyche; you grieve and heal and discover things about yourself you never knew. And this is the truth: your writing really does get better.

MAKE A COMMITMENT
BY MAKING THE TIME

Talking about writing isn't the same as writing. Anyone who has promised herself she'd go to the gym today "no matter what" then finds herself still in her office clothes at 10 PM knows this. "I'll do it tomorrow," the would-be exerciser says day after day, just like the would-be writer.

The way to make a commitment to writing practice is to make an appointment with your writer-self and keep it — same as you would an appointment with your dentist or your best friend or the personal trainer you signed up with at the gym. Write in your daily calendar the amount of time each day that you plan to write. Try to set aside at least half an hour; an hour is even better. Write it down. Then do it.

Getting into a regular practice groove may take a few test runs. You may schedule mornings when nights are really better. If you commit to two hours every day but find yourself stressed-out and

> I believe that the act of writing is itself the muse.
>
> ⟨ BRET ANTHONY JOHNSTON ⟩

hating the idea of writing practice and going to the page with a Godzilla-sized grudge, or, worse yet, not going at all, reconsider how much time you can really commit. Be flexible. Create a schedule that works for you, so that when practice time comes, you accept it as an ongoing, necessary part of your life as a writer and look forward to it as a gift to yourself.

You may have to change your appointment. Certainly there will be days when, no matter what, you simply have to cancel. When this happens, do it consciously and with intention. Just as you would call your dentist or best friend to reschedule rather than standing them up, tell yourself why you have to postpone or change the appointment, and set a time for another meeting. Your writer-self deserves this consideration.

WRITING PRACTICE PROMPTS

Many writing practitioners, when they sit down to write, freeze. "I don't know what to write about," they say, while holding the pen in a death grip somewhere down near the nib, or while their fingers hover over their keyboard like so many hummingbirds. Truth is, each of us has so much we want to write about, a deluge of ideas, memories, and images, that we can become paralyzed by infinite choice. The brain simply can't make up its mind, so it launches into what it does best: measuring, judging, calculating. Thinking. The worst possible thing for writing practice.

This is why I've included suggested writing topics, or prompts, for each day of the year. The prompts are located on the bottoms of pages sprinkled throughout the book. To use this book, simply locate the date, write the prompt for that day at the top of a blank page in your notebook, grab the first image that comes to you, and write it. No matter what the topic, what you want to write about will emerge on the page. Story seedlings, poetic uprisings, character visitations — things that are deep inside are brought to the surface by the focus and energy and freewheeling fearlessness of writing practice.

If you want to time your writings, find the day's prompt, then set your timer for the allotted time. I use a plain old kitchen timer; those more tech savvy use the alarms on their iPhones or BlackBerries.

When you write from a prompt, feel free to change the tense — past to present or vice versa — or the point of view. If the prompt uses "you," it doesn't mean you have to write about yourself. Change the pronoun to "he" or "she," or use a character's name (or a real person, if you want). Use the prompts to write from a character's point of view, create a fragment, or work on a scene for a longer piece. Write fiction, memoir, essay. Mix the genres; find your writer's groove, then ride it.

The writing topics are expressed in several ways — as sentence stems, quotes, directives, or simply phrases or words. For example, the topic for January 24 is a simple, straightforward directive: *Write about a summer garden*. If the first image that comes to you is a garden you planted with your father when you were six years old, write about that garden. Begin with the feel of the warm sun on your back as you bent to dig with your little shovel, the texture of the dark earth in your hands, and how little grains of it got under your fingernails. Keep going with specific details that bring the memory alive. Or you can write a fictional piece — put your character in a summer garden where she is hoeing weeds while remembering how her boyfriend cheated on her. Write an essay about gardens, your own or someone else's, and how tomatoes taste when you pick them, still sun-warm, from the vine. Describe a photograph or painting of a garden. Write a garden poem. The places you can go with this prompt are as varied as the types of beans you can plant.

The topic for April 17 is a sentence stem: *"Moving into the new house . . ."* Because the prompt is set in quotation marks, it invites you to use the sentence as dialogue, but you don't have to. Simply begin with the sentence stem, follow the last word with the first image that comes to you, and take the next fifteen minutes to write about a new house, or the mess of the move, or how you (or your character) had to go to the chiropractor after lifting that sofa. You don't even have to write about a house or moving. You can change the order of the words: "You said moving into the new house wouldn't take more than two days." And go from there. Or anywhere.

June 29 offers a line from a poem by Henri Michaux: *"I am writing you from a far-off country."* Throughout the book, other writers are quoted, sometimes, as in this case, with a line for a writing prompt. When writing from this prompt, it's not necessary to actually use the line in your writing. Use instead the images it suggests — of far-off countries that arise from your memory or in your imagination, or the country you'd like to be in as you write. Of course, you can use the line anywhere in the piece, even as a line of dialogue or the lead-in to start your writing.

You're traveling. You're not alone is the prompt for October 22. This topic can be written in the second person (addressing "you"), or it can be about yourself (a memory of traveling), or it can be about a fictional character. Again, run with the image that comes from the prompt, without taking the prompt too literally.

> A writer stays alive because he or she is writing, or may write: the elusive divine exists.
>
> ⌒ JAYNE ANNE PHILLIPS ⌒

One more example: the topic for January 23 is *Nearing midnight*. The lack of any directive (*write about, describe, remember*) is intentional. You're free to use the actual words as the beginning of a sentence, or to find inspiration in the idea of "nearing midnight" as a time, space, feeling, or image. Or write a "nearing midnight" memory.

Prompts aren't themes for compositions or essays. They're not topics you must stay with, as in "stick to the topic." The idea is not to think about what the prompts mean or how to interpret them. Just start writing. The freedom to let your writing go down any open road is one of the delights of writing to suggested prompts. You don't even have to use the prompt itself!

Different writers respond to different invitations. Some writers resonate with concrete images; others like abstract. And often, the less said about a prompt, the more wide-open the invitation for the intuitive to work. A sentence stem one day, an evocative quote the next, sometimes just an image —

this variety stimulates writerly interest and keeps the prompts fresh. Don't worry about "doing it right." The good news is, there's no way to do it wrong. Simply read the prompt, trust the image, and begin writing.

You can use the same prompts again and again; different images will emerge, memories will rise, fresh ideas will form, and you'll keep writing. After some time, you'll be able to reread your notebooks and notice themes and recurring images. This is another gift of writing practice: you'll discover what matters to you as a writer, what you're passionate about.

An important note about the prompts: Don't reject a prompt out of hand or consider what you're going to write about before you begin. Find the day's prompt, note it at the top of your page, and begin writing. If you stop to think, you'll run the risk of talking yourself out of what might be a rich vein for writing practice mining.

THE BOOK OF DAYS

The book is divided into months, with each of the twelve months containing a profusion of counsel and advice, words of inspiration, and literary lore and legend. Each month begins with one of twelve "Guidelines for Writing Practice" that are just that: guidelines to help you along the writing practice road. Some of these may sound familiar. Concepts like "Keep writing" and "Don't worry about the rules" are presented in any number of books on the craft. They're not original, but they are basic to creating a solid foundation on which to build your daily work.

You'll also find hundreds of rousing exercises on everything from auditioning words to using your dreams in your writing. You'll find out how to build your own writing community and how to say yes to the Muse. Tips and how-tos help you discover places to practice, reveal what matters to you as a writer, and show you how to translate real life into fiction. Easy-to-use checklists expose the telltale signs that let you know when the critic, the censor, or the editor is having its way with your writing. Subjects are cross-referenced so you can easily find related information.

Throughout the book, the experience, wisdom, opinions, and even a few quirks and idiosyncrasies of a number of well-known writers are presented in "The Writing Life." This monthly feature brings to the fore such unlikely information as how these writers courted the Muse, what they dreamed about, and how they supported themselves on their way to becoming full-time writers.

Closing out each month is "Beyond Practice" — special invitations for writers to treat themselves. Consider these a reward. A bonus, if you will. Dividends for hard work and hanging in. With titles such as "Café Writing," "On the Road," "Hot Nights/Wild Women," and "A Jug of Wine, a Loaf of Bread — a Notebook," these twelve self-directed mini-workshops encourage writing practitioners to set aside a once-a-month special session to honor themselves as writers and nourish the writing-self. Alone or with the friendly company of other writers, the sessions take participants outside the margins of daily practice and into the wider world that exists beyond practice. Use these sessions to have fun, to play, to expand possibilities, and to explore the further reaches. Evocative in and of itself, each session features a handful of bonus writing prompts. Enjoy.

> For me, writing is like breathing.
>
> ⌒ HARUKI MURAKAMI ⌒

THE EFFECTS OF WRITING PRACTICE

For over seventeen years, I've been leading writing practice groups, sometimes two or three a week, and writing marathons that run long hours, and I always write along with the others. I have also participated in countless practice sessions alone, with various writing partners, and with a mélange of writing groups. Here's what I know:

On any given day, a writer can write the best she's ever written, or she can compose a piece that's clunky and misshapen and downright embarrassing in its black-and-white awfulness. Practice isn't about being a good writer or a bad writer; it's about being present with the writing, surrendering to the process, and trusting the pen.

At any given practice session, we all start with the same thing — the blank page.

Through writing practice, I have been invited to participate in a community where I am free to be all that I am as writer — insecure, self-conscious, ungraceful, passionate, raw, reckless, wild, and even outside my self. I have found my own kind.

By showing up at the page and doing the writing, I, and other writers, have filled hundreds of notebooks. We have started and completed short stories, plays, novels, essays, memoirs, and gifts of writing for others, and, wondrously, we have even experienced the appearance of poems. We've claimed ourselves as writers.

If you will practice every day, and be gentle with yourself, you may be amazed. Your writing will be fresher, livelier, more spontaneous. You will take more risks, write more passionately, and reach into places you didn't know existed. Ideas and images and language with brilliant plumage will parade on the page before your eyes. Then one day, after a particularly surprising session, you will read what you have written, shake your head in astonishment, and say, "Where did that come from?" And you will know, it came from you.

Guidelines for Writing Practice

1. **Keep writing.** Don't stop to edit, to rephrase, to think. Don't go back and read what you've written until you've finished.
2. **Trust your pen.** Go with the first image that appears.
3. **Don't judge your writing.** Don't compare, analyze, criticize.
4. **Let your writing find its own form.** Allow it to organically take shape into a story, an essay, a poem, dialogue, an incomplete meander.
5. **Don't worry about the rules.** Don't worry about grammar, syntax, punctuation, or sentence structure.
6. **Let go of expectations.** Let your writing surprise you.
7. **Kiss your frogs.** Remember, this is just practice. Not every session will be magic. The point is to just suit up and show up at the page, no matter what.
8. **Tell the truth.** Be willing to go to the scary places that make your

hand tremble and your handwriting get a little out of control. Be willing to tell your secrets.

9. **Write specific details.** Your writing doesn't have to be factual, but the specificity of the details brings it alive. The truth isn't in the facts; it's in the details.

10. **Write what matters.** If you don't care about what you're writing, neither will your readers. Be a passionate writer.

11. **Read your writing aloud** after you've completed your practice session. You'll find out what you've written, what you care about, when you're writing the truth, and when the writing is "working."

12. **Date your page and write the topic at the top.** This will keep you grounded in the present and help you reference pieces you might want to use in something else.

{ JANUARY }

Eighty percent of success is showing up.
— WOODY ALLEN

KEEP WRITING

The most important part of writing practice is writing, getting the words down on the page. Don't stop to edit, to think, to rephrase, or to rewrite. If you keep your writing hand moving, you'll bypass the censor, the editor, the critic, and if you're lucky, maybe even the ego.

This isn't to say writing practice is "stream-of-consciousness" writing where you attempt to get down every thought that passes through your mind and the writing that emerges is a jumble of disconnected thoughts and images. During practice sessions, stay focused on the topic and the image that arises, and keep the pen moving as it explores that image and then moves on to the next. Sometimes you'll rocket through the topic on a surge of power that started at liftoff and keeps you at warp speed the whole ride; other times your writing will be more like a lazy river on a Sunday afternoon, peaceful and easy and sun-dappled. The trick is to, at any speed, just keep writing till the end.

Don't stop to reread what you've written until you've completed the practice session. Each time you stop, you move out of the place of intuitive trusting to a cerebral place of judging, evaluating, comparing. There is a time for that, but not during practice sessions. Writing practice is for writing.

Just keep the pen moving until the time is up, or until you feel complete.

HOW TO START

You've set aside the time, you're sitting in the place you've chosen to do today's practice session, and you're comfortable. Maybe you're with a writing friend. Pen and notebook are at hand, and you're ready to begin writing. Here's what you do:

> 1. Proceed slowly and take care.
> 2. To ensure that you proceed slowly, write by hand.
> 3. Write slowly and by hand only about subjects that interest you.
>
> ⸙ ANNIE PROULX ⸙

Date your page, find the topic for today's session, and write it at the top of your page. Then, before you start to think about how you want to approach the topic, simply grab the tail of the first image that sailed into your mind when you wrote it down, and begin writing. Let the words spill from your pen easily and naturally. Don't worry about staying in the lines; don't worry about spelling, punctuation, or grammar. Don't worry about anything. Just write. When you come to a natural slowdown, ease your grip on your pen (you may be surprised at how tightly you're holding on). Breathe. Let the next image come to you. It may be an extension of the first image, or it may be something new that was born out of what you've been writing. Whatever image appears, don't resist. Just fall into it, and keep writing.

Above all else, don't stop to think and don't go back and reread what you've written. If you can't think of the name of a place or a person or some other fact, make up something or draw a line. If you run into a blank wall, rewrite the topic, repeat the last line you wrote, or write, "I don't know what to write next." If you keep the pen moving, you'll find your place again. Just keep writing until the time is up or until you feel complete. If you can, read your piece aloud after you've finished (*see* Guideline 11, p. 199).

> Inspiration is wonderful when it happens but the writer must develop an approach for the rest of the time. The wait is simply too long.
>
> ⸙ LEONARD BERNSTEIN ⸙

Congratulate yourself. You honored your commitment to practice and, by doing so, you honored yourself as writer. If it didn't go as smoothly as you wanted, don't worry. There's always tomorrow. And tomorrow and tomorrow.

TOOLS FOR WRITING PRACTICE

Despite the proliferation of computers, especially lightweight laptops, and the ease of composing on them, writing practice is best done by hand (more on this below). Tools for the writer, then, are simple: pen and paper. Inexpensive, portable, and replenishable. Some writers can be downright obsessive about their tools — only a certain paper, a particular pen; anything else and they're off their game. Edwidge Danticat orders flimsy blue exam books from an online office supply store, sometimes using up to one hundred of them for a draft. Amitav Ghosh insists on a black ink Pelikan pen and white, lined paper manufactured in France. I'm a wide-ruled, spiral-bound, three-hole-punched notebook and Pilot Precise V7 fine point, blue ink woman.

Consider this: In a writing practice session of fifteen minutes, you might write 450 words, more or less, or three to four pages. You'll do this every day. Up to as many as one hundred pages a month. (The size of your handwriting, the size of the note-book, the length of the practice session — all these are factors.) Because of the sheer quantity of paper, most practice writers use inexpensive notebooks. Others like leather-bound journals or blank books that reflect their writing mood or writing persona. Most important, find a notebook you're comfortable with, one that fits your writing style and your budget.

> I don't know what inspiration is. But when it comes I hope it finds me working.
>
> ⁀ PABLO PICASSO ⁀

Regarding pens or pencils: Remember, you'll be writing along at a fairly good speed; you'll want a pen that doesn't skip or resist the paper, or bleed through to the other side. Always have a spare. Nothing is more frustrating than to run out of ink in the midst of it all.

{
JANUARY	1	Things that enter by way of silence (after Mark Strand)
JANUARY	2	Write about ashes
JANUARY	3	You're in a courtyard
JANUARY	4	Walls the color of tears
JANUARY	5	Someone cheated
}

WHY WRITE BY HAND

Ah, what technology has brought us! First the typewriter, then the word processor, next the computer, now voice-recognition computers, and laptops that weigh less than a good-sized paperback and are getting smaller and lighter all the time. Why write by hand when there's all this technology, a nanosecond's response to the flick of the finger, the ability to alter sentences, relocate paragraphs, erase, or rearrange whole chapters with macro magic? And how our fingers fly. At last we can almost keep up with our thoughts. With all this, why still write by hand?

> I always have the sense that the words are coming out of my body, not just my mind. I write in longhand and the pen is scratching the words onto the page. I can even hear the words being written.
>
> ⌒ PAUL AUSTER ⌒

Legions of writers still do, and for their own good reasons. For example: Writer bell hooks said there's something about handwriting that slows the idea process. When working on the computer, she said, "You don't have those moments of pause that you need." Spalding Gray believed that writing by hand was the closest thing he could get to his breath, and Anne Tyler said the muscular movement of putting down script on the paper gets her imagination back in the track where it was. Clive Barker said that for him, handwriting is "the most direct association I can make between what's going on in my mind's eye and what's going to appear on the page."

The following are more reasons to write by hand.

- Writing is a physical act; you should do it with your body.
- Writing muscles include the hand and the heart.
- Writing by hand is sensual; it allows you to feel the movement of pen against paper.

TIP OF THE MONTH

Do be kind to yourself. Fill pages as quickly as possible; double space, or write on every second line. Regard every new page as a small triumph.

— RODDY DOYLE

- You can feel your heart beat when you write by hand; sometimes you can feel your pulse in your fingers.
- Writing by hand allows you to write with your breath.
- When you write by hand you slow down enough to write only *some* of your thoughts. In writing practice, more is not necessarily better.
- You are more connected to your feelings when you write by hand.
- Handwriting is alive.
- You are in control when you write by hand (no low battery, malfunction, SAVE command, or crash can interrupt you).
- You can write anywhere when you write by hand.

> Pen or pencil, write with what gives you the most sensual satisfaction.
>
> ⌒ RICHARD HUGO ⌒

Writing by hand is elemental to writing practice. Even if you feel most at home at your computer, fingers flinging words onto the screen, I urge you to slow down, pick up what John Updike called "the humblest and quietest of weapons, a pencil," and try a month's worth of practice writing by hand.

JANUARY 6   Write about the passing of hours

JANUARY 7   Write where the road leads

JANUARY 8   On the horizon

JANUARY 9   The sound of silence (after Simon & Garfunkel)

JANUARY 10   Shapes like stars

THE WRITING LIFE

DESKS AND SPACES

RITA DOVE said she loves the absolute quiet of her cabin in the woods. It's "the silence of the world," she said, "birds shifting weight on branches, the branches squeaking against other twigs, the deer *hooosching* through the woods."

RUSSELL BANKS also has a cabin in the woods, a converted sugar shack that was once used for boiling maple syrup. This is where he scribbles out his first drafts in longhand.

AMY TAN surrounds herself with objects that carry a personal history — old books, bowls, boxes, and chairs and benches from imperial China.

> You don't even need an actual desk. You can be at a desk on the subway. You can be at a desk in the bathroom stalls. Wherever you give yourself over again to sustained meditation.
>
> ◦ JOSHUA FERRIS ◦

RICHARD FORD's desk is more of a concept than a thing. "It's like the 'Belize desk' at the State Department; an idea more than a place you actually sit at."

ANNIE DILLARD recommended a room with no view, "so imagination can meet memory in the dark."

KURT VONNEGUT used his hardwood floor as a "desk" where he spread and piled and kept things near at hand as he worked from his lap while seated on a padded Danish walnut easy chair.

JUNOT DÍAZ retreats to the bathroom and sits on the edge of the tub when he needs to seal himself off from the world.

The bed served as desk for any number of writers, including **WALKER PERCY, EDITH WHARTON, COLETTE, MARCEL PROUST,** and **JAMES JOYCE.**

"Our task," wrote **JOHN UPDIKE,** "is to rise above the setting, with its comforts and distractions, into a relationship with our ideal reader."

HOW TO CREATE A SPACE OF YOUR OWN

Every writer needs a place to call her or his own, whether it's a folding table behind a screen in the bedroom or a separate studio with desk, computer, napping couch, and window with a view. Find yours and claim it. Furnish it with those things that give you comfort, inspire you, support you. Make it a safe space, a place you go to joyfully. Writing is creating and creating is work/play for the soul.

Your writing space doesn't have to be a fixed location, nor does it have to be the only place you write. Throughout this book are suggestions to make your writing mobile. More than a few writers need the stimulation of public places to get their writing done, especially first-draft writing. At a workshop, Naomi Epel talked about schlepping her grocery cart loaded with laptop, manuscript, reference books, and pages of notes to cafés all over Berkeley. John

> This is where I place myself when I write. I am the Fool about to set off the edge of the world, unafraid of the fall.
>
> ⮌ SUSAN POWER ⮌

Wray wrote *Lowboy*, which takes place in the New York City subway, while actually on the subway. Writers I know set themselves up in cafés, on airplanes, in their neighborhood library, or out in nature — at the beach, for example. Even individuals who come to weekly writing practice groups have claimed squatter's rights to their own space at the table and always sit in the same chair with the same accoutrements of water bottle or caffe latte or rainbow of pens arrayed before them.

What you need in a writing space is safety and comfort, both psychic and physical: a place where you feel free to lose yourself in the world you are creating on paper.

An idea: spend a practice session describing your ideal writing space, then compare this dreamed-of niche with your current space. What's the same? What can you change to bring the real more in line with the wished-for?

{*See also* Places to Practice, p. 68; Practice Accoutrements, p. 171}

BELIEF & TECHNIQUE FOR MODERN PROSE — LIST OF ESSENTIALS

BY JACK KEROUAC

1. Scribbled secret notebooks, and wild typewritten pages, for yr own joy
2. Submissive to everything, open, listening
3. Try never get drunk outside yr own house
4. Be in love with yr life
5. Something that you feel will find its own form
6. Be crazy dumbsaint of the mind
7. Blow as deep as you want to blow
8. Write what you want bottomless from bottom of the mind
9. The unspeakable vision of the individual
10. No time for poetry but exactly what is
11. Visionary tics shivering in the chest
12. In tranced fixation dreaming upon object before you
13. Remove literary, grammatical and syntactical inhibition
14. Like Proust, be an old teahead of time
15. Telling the true story of the world in interior monolog
16. The jewel center of interest is the eye within the eye
17. Write in recollection and amazement for yourself
18. Work from pithy middle eye out, swimming in language sea
19. Accept loss forever
20. Believe in the holy contour of life
21. Struggle to sketch the flow that already exists intact in mind
22. Dont think of words when you stop but to see picture better
23. Keep track of every day the date emblazoned in yr morning
24. No fear or shame in the dignity of yr experience, language & knowledge
25. Write for the world to read and see yr exact pictures of it
26. Bookmovie is the movie in words, the visual American form
27. In Praise of Character in the Bleak inhuman Loneliness
28. Composing wild, undisciplined, pure, coming in from under, crazier the better
29. You're a Genius all the time
30. Writer-Director of Earthly movies Sponsored & Angeled in Heaven

WRITER'S NOTEBOOKS

Every writer needs one. This is the place you put all that stuff that comes to you while you're focused on something else. It's the workbench for cobbling together bits and pieces or fixing part of your story that is not working.

A writer's notebook is the receptacle for ideas and trying out words and images. A place for making notes to yourself.

Some writers keep separate notebooks for recordings of the senses, descriptions of the weather, character sketches, bits of dialogue, and other subjects. They write everything down in their current, working notebook, then from time to time, transfer pieces into the separate notebooks. These they file on a shelf near their desk. When they need a description of an August sky in Aspen, they finger through their Landscapes notebook till — voilà! — just the entry that works: Aspen, August 14, 1997. And there follows the color of sky, the shape of the clouds with metaphor abounding, the sound of shadow on mountain, light footed and nimble.

A writer's notebook is what you always carry with you. Along with your pen. Howard Junker, editor of the literary journal *ZYZZYVA*, describes his pocket-sized version as his "stealth" notebook and suggests you have one, too. Anne Lamott stuffs three-by-five-inch cards in her back pocket for scribbling down whatever comes to her as she walks the dog or is otherwise away from her desk. She also writes on her body, messy but apparently effective. I hope you will take the time to read or reread Joan Didion's essay "On Keeping a Notebook," which appears in her book *Slouching Towards Bethlehem*. Some writers I know keep a supply of prompts in their notebooks in the happy event that they find themselves with a little extra time for an impromptu practice session.

JANUARY 11	Write about falling asleep
JANUARY 12	In the distance
JANUARY 13	When she looked up…
JANUARY 14	Write about "the light of the lamps and candles" (after Ivan Turgenev)
JANUARY 15	Write about an unfamiliar subject

> Always carry a notebook....The short-term memory only retains information for three minutes; unless it is committed to paper you can lose an idea forever.
>
> ⟿ WILL SELF ⟿

Writer's notebooks lean toward the chaotic. Unless they're airlifted out, jottings tend to get recorded and forgotten, like last year's holiday cards. In *Turning Life into Fiction*, Robin Hemley suggests leafing back through your notebook (he calls his a journal) from time to time. As when panning for gold, you might get nuggets and you might get gravel. But then again, you could be making a driveway, and a few loads of gravel might be just what you need.

{
JANUARY 16   The place where wings unfurl
JANUARY 17   What is seen through open windows
JANUARY 18   Write about a sideways glance
JANUARY 19   She was a redheaded woman
JANUARY 20   "An immobile time not marked on clocks"
             (after Charles Baudelaire)
}

DAILY ROUTINE

Imagine that you put off brushing your teeth until you could spend some really serious time doing it, or that every day you waited to drive to work until you felt inspired to do so. Okay, so these are ridiculous comparisons, but the point is, when something is part of your daily routine, you don't struggle with doing it; you simply build it into your schedule and do it. The suggestion here is to make writing a part of your routine — just like brushing your teeth and driving to work.

Benefits of and Variations on the Practice of a Daily Routine

1. Making writing a part of your daily routine means it will be easier to write. Postponing until you can get in some "really good hours" often translates into not writing at all — something always seems to come up. Or the stress of "have to" writing blocks any really good work.

   A daily writing routine means that when those long stretches of writing time — weekends, holidays, vacations — come, you can slip as easily into the time as you slide your feet into your favorite slippers. Plus, you have all that raw material to work with.

   > And how do you learn the craft? In the trenches...I say write and then write and write and write some more and go write some more.
   >
   > ⮞ AUGUST WILSON ⮜

2. When you make an appointment for writing time, you don't have to struggle with the "should" or "ought" of writing, or make the decision to write or not write; you just do it. You honor the appointment with your writer-self as much as you would an appointment with your doctor, your business partner, or your best friend.

3. Just because Ernest Hemingway believed he had to get to work before the sun rose doesn't mean you have to. Set your daily routine for writing at the time that suits you best, not when everyone else says you should.

If you're an early riser, do your writing practice in the morning, when you first awaken. Stay in bed and write under the covers if you want. But if you need a few cups of coffee before you can even hold a pen, by all means have them. Some of us even like to start projects at ten o'clock at night and work into the wee hours. For example, Dan Chaon cranks it out between 11 PM and 4 AM, and Michael Chabon says he can get more writing done between midnight and one o'clock in the morning than any other hour of the day.

> I feel every day I don't write is wasted.
>
> ⮜ TOM GRIMES ⮞

Find a time when the work flows easily and naturally, when you write instead of edit. Make this your practice time.

4. For a change, vary your daily writing time to catch yourself in different moods, with different energy. Especially if you feel yourself or your writing getting into a rut.

Guaranteed: A daily routine that includes writing will have more benefits than you can imagine. Just for starters, (a) the writing will come more easily, (b) you'll write more, (c) your writing will improve, and (d) you'll realize that you are, after all, a writer.

{*See also* The Discipline of Writing, p. 195}

> **JANUARY 21**   Write about saying goodbye
> **JANUARY 22**   You're in a tent
> **JANUARY 23**   Nearing midnight
> **JANUARY 24**   Write about a summer garden
> **JANUARY 25**   A word left unspoken

HOW CAN YOU TELL WHEN IMAGINATION IS PRESENT?

Someone said all you need to be a writer is an imagination and curiosity. (Add to that, stamina.) Your imagination is in the unique, individual way you see the world, the particular and specific details you notice, and the connections you make. More than merely your experience, it is the way you contemplate and interpret your experience. Henry James said, "[Experience] is the very atmosphere of the mind; and when the mind is imaginative . . . it takes to itself the faintest hints of life, it converts the very pulses of air into revelations."

> The imagination has resources and intimations we don't even know about.
>
> ⬿ CYNTHIA OZICK ⬾

How can you tell whether the imagination is present, not only in your writing but also in your life?

- You feel a strong urge to create — to write, to paint, to play music, to dance, to make art.
- Your writing is bold, full of passion and life. "Violent passions emit the Real, Good and Perfect tones," William Blake said.
- You experience great freedom in your writing, leaping from image to image as if your words were Baryshnikov and your notebook the stage.
- You work innocently, not from the ego and not to please or impress.
- You are comfortable doing nothing. For long stretches of time.
- You trust your writing and your experience.
- You live in the present moment because you know that is where imagination will look for you.
- You meander rather than stride calisthenically; you notice the form and colors of leaves, the shape of clouds, the curve of a hill.
- Your writing (and your life) surprises you.
- You try some new thing rather than doing the same old, same old — even if the tried and true was great.
- You believe you will never run out of ideas.

- You don't plan what you are going to do — you just do it; the planning comes later. And even the planning is creative, lively, inspired.
- You go forth (in your writing and your life) with no fear.

> Inside every human being, there is unlimited time and space. In our exterior life, we can be only one person. But in our imagination, we can be anyone, anywhere.
>
> ⌁ JANET FITCH ⌁

- You gaze out windows for long periods of time and stare into treetops; you've been accused of daydreaming.
- You write new, raw, wild stuff instead of rewriting the same piece endlessly.
- You converse about your characters as if they were fully alive.
- You are completely yourself. That's when ideas come, according to Mozart, who knew these things.
- You make up things with the abandon of a child. Spontaneity thrills you.
- You write without the need to prove anything.
- You live your life fully, submerging yourself completely in the experience of it.

You cannot force imagination to be present, but if you are in no hurry, "free, good-natured and at ease," it will appear, according to Brenda Ueland, who said, "The imagination is always searching in us and trying to free what we really think."

{*See also* Gifts from the Muse: Phrases, Images, and Other Kindnesses, p. 133}

BEYOND PRACTICE

A WRITING DATE

Writing with someone else changes the energy of practice sessions. Another person can offer moral support, a friendly ear for your words, and companionship for those times when writing solo is just too lonely. Writing with someone else and reading your work aloud to each other creates a kind of intimacy, a writerly friendship that's unlike any other.

Invite a writing friend or someone you know from a writing workshop for a writing date. Cafés are good meeting places, as are parks or other outdoor settings. The absence of homelife distractions and the benefit of being in neutral territory make public spaces better than individual homes for this sort of date. If you choose a restaurant, make sure the proprietor looks kindly on the lengthy occupation of his table that a writing date implies, and that it's a place where you'll feel comfortable reading aloud to each other. Allow a couple of hours.

Naturally, you'll want to chat first, catch up on any news, and get comfortable in the space and with each other. But set a limit for your chatting. All talking and no writing do not a writing date make.

Each of you can bring three prewritten writing prompts, or jot them down as you prepare to write. Commingle the topics in the center of the table (written on a small strip of paper, folded to conceal the contents); select one at random and write for five minutes. After each person has read aloud what they've written, select another topic and write for ten minutes, then do a fifteen-minute, a ten-minute, and a five-minute session, reading after each writing. Or write on one topic for twenty minutes, then a quickie on another topic for three minutes. Quickie writings of one, two, or three minutes that follow a longer session often offer up writing of surprising depth for such a short length of focused time.

Begin a completely new piece with each prompt or continue the same piece using each new prompt to alter the course of the piece.

Over the forty-five minutes that you write together, you may notice that your partner's writing has informed yours, and vice versa. You may pick up images from each other's writing, and it's not unusual for each person to write an identical or similar image or use the same unique word like *pomegranate* or *grandiose*. Call it coincidence if you want.

> Writing is love, a mission, and a calling, and how and where and why you write are very critical issues.
>
> LYNN SHARON SCHWARTZ

A writing date doesn't have to be limited to two people. Invite three or four for a session. More than five, and it becomes a party rather than a date, and the actual writing may be harder to come by, especially if meals are involved. One group that holds a monthly dinner and writing party insists that writers write before they're fed, once more before they're treated to dessert, and sometimes once again between courses or as a nightcap. It's the literary version of singing for your supper.

Here are some prompts you can use:

- Things you know without asking.
- Write about getting up in the morning.
- Write about stolen moments.
- "I told you stories about . . ."
- Sometimes she forgets what she wants.

{FEBRUARY}

The way to find your true self is by recklessness and freedom.
— BRENDA UELAND

GUIDELINE 2

TRUST YOUR PEN

When you first read a writing practice topic, an image will appear. You can trust this image. Quoting Buddhist master Chögyam Trungpa Rinpoche, Allen Ginsberg reminded us, "First thought, best thought." This first thought comes from your intuitive mind, where the creative process finds its foothold and the ego holds no sway. This is the place of rich images and deep thoughts.

Grasp your pen lightly and let come what wants to come. Follow your pen as it writes the image, word by single word. You may sense some rush to get on to the next image, but there's no hurry. Take a breath and let your pen roam freely within the boundaries of the first image while you ride along. Then write the next image and the next. Out of this, an order will organically arise — one that you would have missed had you rushed headlong from one image to the next.

Ginsberg also said, "It is necessary to resort to some very crude and rapid method of notation to sketch some fleeting sensory detail of this process of myriad sensations running thru the Being. . . . I do not know what I do. I get lost. I tell lies. I follow what comes in my mind next."

The pen is the tool of the intuition. It won't take you further or deeper than you want to go, but it might take you to uncharted places you never thought about consciously.

TIMED WRITINGS

When I first began doing writing practice sessions with other writers, we set a time for our writing, probably to give structure to the session more than anything else. However, over the years, I discovered that setting a time limit has many other beneficial effects than simply creating structure.

1. It becomes easier to actually do the writing ("anybody can write for ten or fifteen minutes").
2. A tension is created that enables you to focus.
3. The writer is allowed to forget himself and be present with the writing.
4. It evokes spontaneity; there's no time to think or ponder.
5. It keeps the writer writing, moving forward to the next word, instead of rewriting, reconsidering, rethinking.
6. With an end in sight, it's easier to begin.
7. There's freedom in knowing you don't have to finish; you just stop when the time is up. Consequently, you can take more risks.
8. Writing time can easily be fit into a too-full schedule.
9. Writing that doesn't work or isn't interesting can be abandoned when the time's up.
10. On the other hand, that same writing can turn interesting if pursued for the full amount of time allotted.

> Writers write. If you can't get to the paper, writing won't occur.
>
> ⌒ GAIL SHER ⌒

It's not necessary to time every practice session, especially when you're writing alone. You may find yourself writing for an hour or more without looking up from the page, and who knows what you might lose if you stop just because of an arbitrary time limit. I say, when you're hot, you're hot, and if you're cooking, keep writing, no matter what.

PAY ATTENTION

Do you remember what you had for breakfast this morning? Can you describe the texture of moonlight on your bedroom ceiling or the face of the old man down the street as he walked his dog? "The truth is in the details," someone once said, and the only way to know the truth is to pay attention.

> Honour the miraculousness of the ordinary.
> ⌒ ANDREW MOTION ⌒

Paying attention brings into focus the specificity not only of good writing but also of mindful living. The great spiritual leader Thich Nhat Hanh said mindfulness is to be present in the present moment. It is in the present moment you find the details that will enrich your writing and bring it to life. "There is ecstasy in paying attention," said Anne Lamott.

As you awaken in the morning, notice the light in your room, the wrinkle of sheets, the smell of air. Be present as you go through your day, mindful of such details as the mist rising from the orange you peel, the ridges of pattern in the peel's color that fade to yellow near the green nub of stem, and the stem's starlike pattern.

Notice what you notice, take the high points, and write them down in your notebook. Create word sketches of gesture, sound, color, texture. By paying attention to what you notice, you begin to see how the writer in you views the world and relationships. These recorded word pictures validate the world you see and experience. By paying attention and writing what you perceive, you find your own truth, and this is what you will pass on in your writing.

{*See also* Truth Is in the Details, p. 54; Slow Down, p. 85; Hunting and Gathering, p. 152}

TIP OF THE MONTH

Let go of everything when you write, and try at a simple beginning with simple words to express what you have inside.

— NATALIE GOLDBERG

WRITE FROM THE SENSES

The senses provide a physical world for our writing as well as a palette for rich imagery and language. It's through the five senses that we ground our writing in the concrete — the sight, sound, smell, taste, and feel of it — moving out of our heads and into our bodies. Words and descriptions reach out from the page and into the sensory perceptions of the reader, and the piece comes to life for him.

> The beginning of human knowledge is through the senses and the fiction writer begins where human perception begins.
>
> ⌁ FLANNERY O'CONNOR ⌁

Within the realm of the senses are born metaphor and simile. One thing is another; something is like something else. Imagery emerges from the chrysalis of sensuous language and takes wing.

As you write, pause to take a sensory inventory. Close your eyes and breathe in the smell of the place you're writing, listen to its sounds, reach out and feel the textures, taste the air, the wind, the rain. You are looking not for words, but, as Jack Kerouac put it, "to see the picture better" — the colors, the shapes and textures of it, the way the light falls upon the bricks, the shadows of doorways, the movement of fog over river.

- Begin writing practice sessions with "I remember the smell of . . . I remember the taste of . . . I remember the feel of . . . I remember the sound of . . . I remember the sight of . . ." Focusing on one sense, capture in three or four short sentences the first image that comes to you, collecting specific details as you go. As you put the concluding period on your first paragraph, but before you stop to think of another memory, write "I remember [the same sense] . . ." again and catch the next image. You may be surprised by the images that appear and the memories that are evoked, especially if you keep your pen moving and don't stop to try and remember.

  Fill a page with four or five short memories, then choose one and do an expanded writing from it, starting with the memory as you first wrote it, or enter the memory from another vantage point. Keep the rest of your list for later practice sessions.

  You can do these sensory "I remember . . ." exercises again and again; you're almost guaranteed a new set of memories each time. If one image continues to reappear, you can be certain it is one that wants to be written about. Honor it by writing it.

- Create pages in your notebook for litanies of smells, tastes, textures, colors, shapes, sounds. Continue to weed out clichés as they sprout. When you come upon one, rework it to make it fresh. {*See also* Clichés and Other Bad Habits, p. 164}
- Describe a place using only sight, only smell, only sound, only taste, only touch.
- Play with synesthesia — the description of one kind of sense impression that uses words that normally describe another: a sound becomes a color, a smell becomes a sound, an emotion becomes a taste. For example, the saxophone sound of midnight; the taste of yesterday, yellowed and brittle; T. S. Eliot's "violet hour." See how many of the senses you can find in "a brassy blonde," or "a buttery sun." (For more on synesthesia, see *A Natural History of the Senses*, by Diane Ackerman, a reference book that's written like poetry and ought to be on every writer's bookshelf.)

> I would ask my students to always be aware of the sensual world, the breathing, smelling illuminated world.
>
> ⮞ PETER CAREY ⮜

- Take a sensory tour of your bed, your desk, your room, your house, your backyard. Sit for a time with your notebook and write your perceptions as an artist who continues to look from subject to page, sketching in details, then going back for more.
- Pause throughout the day to notice sensory details. Even if you don't write them in your notebook, this will put you in touch with your body and keep sensory details present in your mind, which means they'll be more present in your writing.

FEBRUARY 1   Her button was undone
FEBRUARY 2   Through a crack in the door
FEBRUARY 3   Write about "The instrument of the sorrowful" (after Stéphane Mallarmé)
FEBRUARY 4   Write a twilight memory
FEBRUARY 5   Someone is reading a poem

AUDITIONING WORDS

This is how important words are: Imagine you're a director and you're casting words for your next production. You could say "the plot's the thing" and any old words that tell the story will work just fine. That would be like casting Goofy as Richard III, or Miss Piggy as Blanche DuBois. "The difference between the right word and almost the right word is the difference between lightning and a lightning bug," said Mark Twain.

Audition your words. Go for better. Don't settle for *red* when *crimson* is the word you want. If not *crimson*, what about *carmine, scarlet, garnet*? Let *a whisper* be *a murmur, a snuffle, a soft lament*.

Read your words out loud and listen for the rhythm, the repeated sounds, the slant rhymes that happen inside as you string (chain, tier, caravan) the words together. Study poetry for its rhythm and musicality. Author and teacher Gary Provost wrote, "Writing is not a visual art. It is a symphony, not an oil painting. It is the shattering, not the glass. It is the ringing, not the bell. The words you write make sounds, and when the sounds satisfy the reader's ear, your writing works."

> Every word a writer writes has as its purpose a function of truth in that it is a choice — each word eliminates an endless number of possibilities.
>
> ⌒ SUSANNA MOORE ⌒

As you read other writers, notice words and the certain coincidence of words that excite you; write these words in your notebook. Use them in your daily writing practice. Become a connoisseur of words. A wordsmith, honing and crafting the language into art.

{*See also* Wordplay, p. 202; About Language, p. 48; Better Verbs, Fewer Adverbs, p. 134}

FEBRUARY 6	Write about bad blood
FEBRUARY 7	Eating out
FEBRUARY 8	Living as he did…
FEBRUARY 9	Counting his (her) breaths
FEBRUARY 10	The skin on her cheek

SELF-SABOTAGE

Sometimes writers undermine their best writing intentions, often without being aware of how they are harming themselves and their writer's spirit. Following is a list of some of the ways you can sabotage yourself and your work.

- Not keeping appointments with yourself to write.
- Allowing others' needs/wants/schedules to interfere with your writing time.
- Allowing people you don't trust to read your writing.
- Comparing your first-draft writing to someone else's finished, published piece.
- Not completing pieces. Stopping when the going gets tough or things get uncomfortable, or when you feel stuck.

> Very few writers really know what they are doing until they've done it.
>
> ⌐ ANNE LAMOTT ⌐

- Believing there is such a thing as perfect. Perfectionism is the number one enemy of all creative efforts!
- Setting standards too high, making goals too lofty: to write for three hours every day when a half hour is more realistic; setting out to write a novel without knowing any of the basics of the craft; simply starting at chapter one, page one.
- Holding unrealistic expectations: to write a novel in three months; complete a short story in a single sitting; write a finished essay in the first draft.
- Believing that if a piece is rejected, it isn't good. Or worse, that you aren't any good. Taking no for an answer. Letting one person's subjective opinion be the ultimate judgment of a piece.
- Sending out material that isn't ready. Not doing research, and then sending the right piece to the wrong publisher.
- Believing that publication means success.
- Writing and working in a vacuum. You need other writers, other opinions.

Most self-sabotaging behavior comes out of fear — fear of claiming our writer-self, fear of disappointing others or of not getting approval or acceptance, fear of success. "Our deepest fear is not that we are inadequate. Our deepest fear is that we are powerful beyond measure," wrote Marianne Williamson. When you begin to honor your writing-self, saying "Yes!" to all you are, self-sabotage will disappear.

{*See also* Honor Yourself as Writer, p. 129; Find Support for Your Writing Life, p. 234}

{
FEBRUARY 11   Driving a gravel road
FEBRUARY 12   Write about an eclipse
FEBRUARY 13   What was seen through binoculars
FEBRUARY 14   Someone is whistling
FEBRUARY 15   Write about animal dreams
}

THE DIFFERENCE BETWEEN WRITING PRACTICE AND JOURNAL WRITING

Writing practice and journal writing have much in common; however, they are two very different processes. Writing practice is focused, creative writing on a topic; journaling is writing for self-exploration, self-expression, and, often, catharsis. While both might be freewheeling and personal, one can be considered public writing and the other, private.

Journal writing techniques focus on going within, writing feelings, reflections, thoughts, and opinions, and provide a forum for processing emotions that arise from introspection. A journal is a place for recording a life, safekeeping memories, dwelling within, and working through. We write to know and express ourselves.

Writing practice is about finding our voices and telling our stories in a creative way — using the craft of writing and the expressive channels of language, imagery, metaphor. We invent and fictionalize, compress and exaggerate. We employ the tools of the craft: dialogue, setting, point of view, mood. Characters are invited in and booted out without regard to "what really happened." We lie to get at the truth and board flights of fancy that transport us to the outer edges of our imaginations. We practice to express ourselves and to get better at our craft.

> One of the things that happens when you give yourself permission to start writing is that you start thinking like a writer. You start seeing everything as material.
>
> ⌒ ANNE LAMOTT ⌒

This is not to say that journal writing cannot be a creative act. Often imaginative, creative writing is found within the sacred pages of personal journals and can be lifted whole and transplanted into a story, essay, or novel. And, for certain, writing practice pieces can help us process and heal, lead us inward on roads otherwise not taken. Expose us to ourselves.

In writing about her journal keeping, Sue Grafton said, "The journal serves as a place to offload anxiety, a verbal repair-shop when my internal writing machine breaks down." Countless writers use their journals in much the same way that I suggest keeping a writer's notebook — the journal as "capacious holdall," in the words of Virginia Woolf, where story ideas,

> I write entirely to find out what I'm thinking, what I'm looking at, what I see and what it means. What I want and what I fear.
>
> — JOAN DIDION

overheard dialogue, bits of poems, quotes, clippings from newspapers and magazines, all manner of notes to self are written down. Several anthologies have been published about writers and their notebooks or journals, including *Writers and Their Notebooks*, edited by Diana Raab, *The Writer's Notebook: Craft Essays from Tin House*, and *The Writer's Notebook*, edited by Howard Junker. And the published journals of many writers — from Virginia Woolf to May Sarton, Anaïs Nin, John Cheever, and others — are viewed as literature. Perhaps most famous of all is *The Diary of Anne Frank*.

Journal keeping and writing practice are not at odds with one another. In fact, they complement each other. Within the journal we find evocative topics to rummage through in practice sessions; during writing practice we touch upon tender places that we may want to explore within the private confines of our journals.

Though some writers like to use the same notebook for journaling and writing practice, a separate notebook for each is recommended. This holds back the tendency to journalize during writing practice and to choose the creative over the introspective in the journal.

FEBRUARY 16	A jewel
FEBRUARY 17	Black as a crow's wing
FEBRUARY 18	Write about picking fruit
FEBRUARY 19	"Everything became shadow" (after Arthur Rimbaud)
FEBRUARY 20	Stolen goods

THE WRITING LIFE

INVOKING THE MUSE

Attend a book signing or talk by a successful author, and when it comes to the Q&A part, you're likely to hear the question, Where do you get your inspiration? Or some variation thereof. The famous writer might tell us she reads poetry or he takes his dog for a walk. Seldom do we hear revelations such as these:

> There is so much about the process of writing that is mysterious to me, but this one thing I've found to be true: writing begets writing.
>
> ⌖ DORIANNE LAUX ⌖

The poet **FRIEDRICH VON SCHILLER** used to keep rotten apples under the lid of his desk, open it, inhale deeply, and compose.

Tea was the stimulant for **DR. JOHNSON** and **W. H. AUDEN**. Johnson was reported to have frequently consumed twenty-five cups at one sitting. **HONORÉ DE BALZAC** drank fifty cups of coffee in a day.

COLETTE first picked fleas from her cat, then wrote. It's told she had a dozen of them (cats, not fleas).

While writing *The Charterhouse of Parma*, **STENDHAL** began the day by reading two or three pages of the French civil code.

WILLA CATHER read the Bible.

SAMUEL TAYLOR COLERIDGE indulged in two grains of opium before working.

ALEXANDRE DUMAS, the elder, wrote his nonfiction on rose-colored paper, his fiction on blue, and his poetry on yellow. **LANGSTON HUGHES** also used a different kind of paper for each project.

RUDYARD KIPLING insisted on the blackest ink available and fantasized about keeping "an ink-boy to grind me Indian ink."

VOLTAIRE used his lover's naked back as a writing desk.

It's said that **EDGAR ALLAN POE** wrote with his cat on his shoulder, **CHARLES**

BAUDELAIRE kept a bat in a cage on his writing desk, and HENRIK IBSEN kept a pet scorpion on his.

T. S. ELIOT preferred writing when he had a head cold.

PAUL WEST listened nonstop to a sonatina by Ferruccio Busoni as he wrote *The Place in Flowers Where Pollen Rests*, while HART CRANE wrote to Cuban rumbas, Maurice Ravel's *Boléro*, and torch songs.

I'm a light-a-candle-read-a-poem-cup-of-coffee woman. How do you let the Muse know you're ready for a visit?

{
FEBRUARY 21	Write about staying awake
FEBRUARY 22	Write about your lover's pillow
FEBRUARY 23	It was a lie
FEBRUARY 24	In a foreign country
FEBRUARY 25	Write about a long bus ride
}

Ten Daily Habits That Make a (Good) Writer

1. **Eat Healthfully.** Give your body what it really wants so it can support you. You may think it wants caffeine, sugar, or alcohol, but it really wants broccoli and spinach. Eat healthfully for stamina, good health, and the sensory experience of it. (Notice your carrots when you eat them, their color and crunch. Smell that onion; look closely at its layers and textures.) Eat several small meals throughout the day; begin with a good breakfast.

2. **Be Physical.** Remember when your mother warned you about making faces ("your face could freeze that way")? If you're sitting at your desk all hours of the day and night, your whole body could petrify that way. Move it — stretch, exercise, work out. Breathe. It roils the blood and feeds the brain. When you walk, run, bicycle, or swim, you're in touch with the earth (unless you do it in a gym, and in that case, *get outside*). Do it alone so you can pay attention to your body and notice your environment as you glide along.

> Writing is never one thing. It's like running a marathon, juggling balls and cracking walnuts and playing fifteen instruments.
>
> — PETER CAREY

3. **Laugh Out Loud.** You take big breaths when you laugh out loud. Laughing helps rid the body of toxins. So lighten up. Take a break from work, and play with your puppy or your child or your neighbor's child. Look at cartoons; tell a joke; share with friends. Find something funny in the world and let loose belly laughs. Create a playground for the Muse.

4. **Read.** Read as much as you can of the best writers. Read on two levels: one as a reader and one as a writer. Study how other writers use language, how they construct a piece. Notice what you love about certain writers. Try reading aloud (especially poetry) before you write.

5. **Cross-Fertilize.** Experience another art form — music, photography, dance, painting, sculpture, film, theater. Keep open books of art in your writing space, a basketful of postcard art to leaf through. If music distracts you while you write, listen at other

times when you can absorb the music and it is not just a background sound. Visit a museum; walk in a sculpture garden. Let other art evoke your own.

6. **Practice Spirituality.** Take time every day (or several times a day) to consciously go to that place you name Sacred — through prayer, meditation, or simply being mindful and present in the present. Make time for whatever you do that keeps you in touch with your spiritual self.

7. **Pay Attention.** Notice the quality of light, the heft of air, color of sky, faces, clouds, flowers, garbage, graffiti — all of it. Slow down and pay attention. Stop during your walks and examine a leaf. Read the writing in shop windows. Observe people getting on a bus, the bus driver, the stink of the bus exhaust.

8. **Give Back.** Do something good or kind for someone or the planet. Speak to someone you don't know, smile, help a friend (or a stranger), plant a flower, reuse a paper bag, wrap a gift with newspaper, walk instead of driving. Be generous with whatever you have to give.

9. **Connect with Another Writer.** Meet a writing friend for coffee, write a letter to a writer whose work you admire (email counts, but not as much as a real handwritten letter in a real envelope with a real stamp that will arrive in someone's mailbox), make a phone call to a writer friend. Attend a poetry reading, a book signing; take part in a workshop. Write with someone. Go online to a writers' chat room, join an online writers' group, respond to a blog, email a poem to a friend.

> A writer's life is not designed to reassure your mother.
>
> ⬦ RITA MAE BROWN ⬦

10. **Write.** Sometime, someplace, every day, honor your writer-self and spend some time writing.

FEBRUARY 26   In the closet
FEBRUARY 27   Write about a crosswind
FEBRUARY 28   It was a daydream
FEBRUARY 29   "Crossing the bridge..."

WHO READS YOUR WRITING?

Exposing your writing, especially the raw, uncooked stuff of writing practice, can be risky. Handing over a notebook filled with the shaggy evidence of practice sessions to someone who doesn't understand the purpose of practice, or someone who believes it's in your best interest to be critiqued, may not be wise. In fact, even if you're not easily embarrassed, handing over your notebook to anyone is probably not a good choice.

Pieces written during practice sessions are not meant for critique. They're not ready yet. Some of them may never be. This is why, when we read our practice pieces aloud in a group or with a writing buddy, we don't critique. We do it to hear our words and to honor them and the process.

Only after you've rewritten, edited, polished, and generally cleaned up a piece will you want to ask for critique. Even then, family and friends are seldom the best audience. They may feel as if they have to criticize the writing, but they don't know what to criticize

> You're the first audience to your work, and the most important audience.
>
> ⬿ GLORIA NAYLOR ⬿

(*Are you sure you want to name your character Maude? Should this be a comma or a semicolon?*); they may criticize you rather than the writing (*You never were very good at grammar*); or they may think any criticism will hurt your feelings and gush with false accolades (*Gosh, honey, this is just great. Have you thought of sending it to the* New Yorker?). Better to ask someone you can trust — preferably another writer whose work you respect and whom you respect as a person, too.

A good read-and-critique group where you are a regular participant is best. Find one made up of writers at your same level of experience and just beyond, either a peer group or with an instructor with whom you're comfortable. If you can't find listings for such groups via local publications or on the Internet, start your own.

{*See also* How to Start a Writing Practice Group, p. 223; Find Your Tribe: Why Hang Out with Other Writers, p. 173; Find Support for Your Writing Life, p. 234}

BEYOND PRACTICE

SNOWBOUND

(or The Serendipitous Effects of Bad Weather on a Good Writer)

There's six feet of new snow, and outside your window a gauzy shroud of white obliterates any horizon.

Or it's been raining since eight o'clock last night, and it's still coming down. You now understand deluge, monsoon, and torrent.

Or some cosmic cook has overseasoned the soup, and the fog is as thick as bouillabaisse.

Let's just say that, for whatever reason, and through forces outside your control, you're homebound for the day. Consider this a gift. You've been given a writing day, free and clear.

This is a day for snugging in. Think of words like *warm, fuzzy, cozy*. Brew up some cocoa; hot, spiced tea; coffee with warmed milk. A few cookies or some buttered toast won't go astray. Build a crackling fire or, lacking a fireplace, encircle your nest with candles. Get your notebook, your favorite pen, and settle in.

> Writing is a craft. You have to take your apprenticeship in it like anything else.
>
> ⌐ KATHERINE ANNE PORTER ⌐

Warm up with a five-minute writing (prompt: Write about a small thing), then maybe a ten-minute writing (prompt: You are in a garden). Refresh your coffee or tea, give the fire a poke, and encamp yourself again. Release all constraints of time and begin another writing session. Continue writing one of the pieces you've already begun, or start fresh (prompt: "It was Monday morning"). Instead of stopping after fifteen or twenty minutes, keep going. When you come to what might be a stopping place, don't mark a period on the page but instead put a comma and keep writing. Or begin again with a connector such as *then* or *however* or *instead of* or *but* and allow the pen to begin its meanderings anew. Write as long as you want. Let this be a leisurely session; there's no schedule to keep, nothing to do instead of write.

If you've been doing writing practice for some time and have more than a few notebooks filled, this might be a day for rereading your notebooks, discovering what you've created. You may find bits and pieces of stories or personal narrative essays you can begin to pull together to make something larger.

Stay warm. Keep writing. Here are a few more prompts, just in case you need them.

- Write about a mirror
- Write a February memory
- "After all, it wasn't what she expected"
- This is not about . . .
- One Friday night

P.S. It doesn't have to be snowing or raining or foggy for you to give yourself a homebound day. Simply take one. It will be good for any old doldrums — winter or not — that might have crept in.

{MARCH}

Writing is a voyage of discovery.
— NADINE GORDIMER

DON'T JUDGE YOUR WRITING

When writing in real time you're bound to be clumsy sometimes; to repeat yourself; change names; switch gender, tense, or even point of view. To use common words and commit clichés. Never mind. Just keep writing. Remember, you're not editing or revising as you write, or considering what might be a better way to express yourself. What you write in writing practice is the roughest of rough drafts — writing that is pouring directly from the intuitive, too fragile and raw for judgments. Especially your own judgments, because, more likely than not, you are your own harshest critic. As Eleanor Roosevelt said, "No one can do to me what I have not already done to myself."

When writing in a group with other writing practitioners, don't compare, analyze, or criticize this bare, uncooked stuff. Or compare your unfinished, first drafts with the finished, published work of other writers. There comes a time to judge your writing and to ask for critique from others, but it is not during writing practice.

All this may be easier said than done. We tend to rush to judgment, to expect better from ourselves no matter how good or fresh or alive our writing may be. "Nothing you write, if you hope to be any good, will ever come out as you first hoped," said Lillian Hellman. Remember to be your own best friend — nonjudgmental, accepting, tolerant, loving, kind, and patient. And remember to laugh sometimes. At yourself and your writing.

TIP OF THE MONTH

Find your best time of the day for writing and write. Don't let anything else interfere. Afterwards it won't matter to you that the kitchen is a mess.

— ESTHER FREUD

PERFECTIONISM

Perfectionism is an ugly thing, all stiff and rigid with pursed lips and beady little eyes. No one likes perfectionism. It comes from a stingy, mean-spirited place and serves no purpose except to make us feel terrible about ourselves and anything we create.

Perfectionism causes us to hold our pens too tight and reject words and ideas before we get them down. If we do evade perfectionism temporarily, when it finds us again, it orders us to cross out, erase, rewrite anything we have written in its absence.

> I was working on the proof of one of my poems all morning and I took out a comma. In the afternoon I put it back in again.
>
> ⌒ OSCAR WILDE ⌒

Perfectionism would have God recast every sunset and chide Mother Nature for her choice of colors. If everything were left up to perfectionism, nothing would exist. You won't hear perfectionism say, "Ah, this is good." Its entire vocabulary begins with *n* words: *no, not, never.*

Knowing that perfect does not exist, or believing that creations (including ourselves) are perfect in their imperfections, lets us make a thing as good as we can, raising our work to the highest level our abilities allow. Then we are able to call it complete, release it, and move on.

{*See also* How to Tell When the Critic Is Present, p. 90}

MARCH 1	"Lips as red as a licked red candy" (after Vladimir Nabokov)	
MARCH 2	Write about the blues in the night	
MARCH 3	"Memory thick as mud" (after Janet Fitch)	
MARCH 4	A lie someone told you	
MARCH 5	The face of tomorrow	

ABOUT LANGUAGE

Language is more than words. Language is music and rhythm; it is sound, rhyme, and sibilance; it is texture and layers. Art and graffiti. Language is attitude and place, geography and history. Language is family and what you heard at the kitchen table and on the back porch, muffled behind closed doors

> Language is the only homeland.
>
> ⌒ CZESLAW MILOSZ ⌒

and shouted up from stairwells. Language is what you do with words, and it is the silence between the words.

It is impossible, we sometimes think, to convey what we feel or what we want to express in words, those "small shapes in the gorgeous chaos of the world," as Diane Ackerman described them. Yet other times, it is almost as if we are tracing with our pen words that are already in place, near-perfect and exact.

"To say what you want to say, you must create another language and nourish it for years and years with what you have loved, with what you have lost, with what you will never find again," wrote George Seferis.

How to Find and Claim Your Own Language

- Write that which you heard around your childhood kitchen table, in your grandmother's house, when family gathered and stories were told. Write from the prompt "I remember..." to generate images.

- Write stream of consciousness, allowing language that comes from the deep, unconscious place to take shape on your page. Read aloud what you've written to hear the language of your intuitive voice; listen for words, rhythms, sounds. "There is a sense in sounds beyond their meaning," said Wallace Stevens.

- List five scents, sounds, emotions, tastes, textures, things you see. Then create similes (something is like something else) for each item. Do it quickly without thinking too hard. Avoid the easy cliché. Your "something else" will speak in your own language.

- Study authors you love to read and whose language resonates with you. Copy whole passages of their writing into your notebook so you sense the physicality of their language. When you read phrases that make you catch your breath, write them down. Use them as writing prompts for practice sessions.

- Write monologues from the point of view of yourself in different photographs, either real pictures or those you imagine. In a variation of an exercise from Pat Schneider's book *The Writer as an Artist*, give the you in the photo a voice on the page, writing in the first person. Begin with "In this one I am...," or simply begin with the first thought that comes.

- Let music suggest language. Listen to different types of music, from big symphonies to acoustic guitar — classical, jazz, rock, rap, ethnic and world music — and write the language you hear.

- As you read through newspapers or magazines, notice which photographs draw your attention. There is something in these particular pictures that is speaking in your language. Tear out these photos (not the accompanying story or article) and keep them in a folder. As a writing practice exercise, pull one of the pictures and write from it — a monologue from an individual, a dialogue between two or more people, or a story about the subjects. Look long at the image before you begin to "hear" the language that is being spoken.

> I don't believe there is any greater blessing than of being pierced through and through by the splendor and sweetness of words.
>
> ⌒ EDITH WHARTON ⌒

- Write a letter you will never send. This allows you to communicate what you want or need to say to someone in language you might not be able to use in person. For example, you can express your anger to a person whom you would never be able to confront, or you can say good-bye to someone you might not have had closure with, even someone who has died. Such letters use the language of our emotions. In your notebook, make a list of people to whom you want to write a not-to-be-sent letter. Now choose someone from the list and write the letter. Writing such letters not only helps you discover the language of your heart, but can be a very healing experience as well.

- "Language alone protects us from the scariness of things with no name," said Toni Morrison. Use the language of your fears, give voice to your terrors, call them up in the night and name them. Do this, too, with your joys and your pleasures. Write in the language of your prayers.

{*See also* Wordplay, p. 202; Auditioning Words, p. 32; Better Verbs, Fewer Adverbs, p. 134}

MARCH 6	What can be seen through the fog
MARCH 7	Write about your father's eyes
MARCH 8	At the end of an empty street
MARCH 9	"The woman in the window" (after Roger Aplon)
MARCH 10	On the eve of the funeral

A FEW SENTENCES ON THE SENTENCE

In her beautiful book *The Writing Life*, Annie Dillard writes of the well-known writer who got collared by a university student who asked, "Do you think I could be a writer?"

"Well," the writer said, "I don't know. . . . Do you like sentences?"

In the beginning may have been the Word, but to go forward we need lines of words, one after the other, that lead us into the next line of words, and so on and so on to the end of what we have to say. In this journey of one word and then the next, we have created everything — tone, character, action, drama, story. So much depends on how we string together this assemblage of words. Think of pearls and kite tails.

"All you have to do is write one true sentence," said Hemingway.

> Make every sentence you write an event.
>
> ⌒ JOHN DUFRESNE ⌒

Sentences are the basic structure of the language. Every sentence needs a subject and a verb. It can be very simple: She wrote. Or full of convolutions and phrases, clauses, breaks, commas, asides, parenthetical thoughts that can go on and on and still not be a sentence. (For a magnum opus of a nonsentence, read Donald Barthelme's fictional piece, "The Sentence.")

Here are some tips on writing sentences:

1. Put things in logical order so the reader can follow. Make sure you put your words on paper in the order that you want the reader to see the images they represent. Don't show images before the reader sees the action.

2. Put emphatic words at the end. Emphasis tends to flow to the end of a sentence, so if there is a word or phrase you want to say a little more loudly, put it at the end.

3. Put the most powerful sentence at the end of the paragraph so the reader is left with that image during the silence between paragraphs.

4. Vary the length of your sentences. Strings of sentences of all the same length feel repetitive and boring to the reader. Read

through a paragraph of your writing and do a word count in your sentences. One of my all-time favorite paragraphs is the second paragraph in Barbara Kingsolver's book *The Poisonwood Bible*. The word counts of its sentences are 4–12–15–22–11–4–7–23–20–7. (The first paragraph in that book, by the way, is a single-sentence stunner: "Imagine a ruin so strange it must never have happened.") What a sentence says and does determines its length.

5. Vary the construction of your sentences. Use clauses, complex sentences, series; use complete sentences or sentence fragments (but not too often); use punctuation to create breaks and pauses. In *The Art of Fiction*, John Gardner writes of the importance of rhythm in sentences. "By keeping out a careful ear for rhythm, the writer can control the emotion of his sentences with considerable subtlety."

I was once told that every sentence should contain at least one surprising word, a word that packs a wallop. But sometimes when I try for that roundhouse, I use a word that calls too much attention to itself and instead knocks down the whole wobbly structure. The job of the sentence is to lead the reader to the next sentence. Still, in reading some of my favorite writers, I like to get stopped in my tracks by a sentence so stunning, so beautiful, and so true that I don't want to go forward. Not just yet. I want to linger, as if this sentence were a gorgeous painting or sculpture — a work of art, which I believe it is. I hope the same is true for you.

MARCH 11	The world before you were born	
MARCH 12	"These are the seductive voices of the night"	
	(after Franz Kafka)	
MARCH 13	Attending a ceremony	
MARCH 14	Write about fruit flesh	
MARCH 15	This is how lonesome feels	

FALSE STARTS

It may happen during any given practice session. You're on a roll with two or three sentences that feel pretty good, when you're suddenly stopped dead, absolutely unable to continue. Or those two or three roiling sentences cool down to a thin trickle, finally petering out into a desert of bony, dry words. In writing practice, we call this a false start. The image gives out, or you know you've started something you can't sustain. Or two or three sentences in, and you're already boring yourself. These false starts may happen more than once on any given topic. When this occurs, simply drop down a line or two, and start again until you find your groove. Sometimes it may be as simple as restating one of the lines you've already written, coming at it from a slightly different angle or entering through another door. Especially if the image is compelling.

However, it's possible to have a whole day of false starts, when you just can't get into anything. When this happens, it could be that your mind is away on other business and hasn't joined you at the desk, or the stress of your "other" life is keeping you from being present with your writing. Try bringing yourself to the present by taking a few deep breaths and settling into your chair with a simple grounding meditation: Close your eyes and feel the floor beneath your feet, the chair beneath your bottom, the support of your spine. Remind yourself to drop your shoulders, relax your eyes and mouth, and breathe into your body. Then start your writing practice again, using the same prompt, or choosing another. I always have extra prompts stashed away in my notebook. Or start your writing with "I remember..." or "I think..." or "This morning..." and just follow your pen.

> A writer is a man who, embarking upon a task, does not know what to do.
>
> DONALD BARTHELME

Note: The urge to avoid a path because it's scary or feels out of control isn't the same as a false start.

{*See also* Take Risks, p. 132; Avoiding the Truth, p. 98}

TRUTH IS IN THE DETAILS

Details, truthfully rendered, bring your writing to life and create connection points for the reader. It is from these connection points — a red damask table-cloth with a gravy stain, the maître d' with a mole above his lip where a thick, black hair protrudes, Hemingway's woman with "eyes as dark as wet black currants" — that a world emerges. Using the writer's specific details as a run-way, the reader's imagination can soar into the universe of the story.

Single, telling details skillfully wrought relate more about a character or a place than a thousand more general aspects. For example, "She would never go to California; she needed to stay in a place where she knew the names of the trees," or "At forty-eight, she's had only one serious relationship in her life and has never owned her own washer and dryer."

> We think in generalities, but we live in detail.
> ⌐ ALFRED NORTH WHITEHEAD ⌐

As you write, reach out to grab the tail of a detail — the color of sky, smell of air, objects within your sight. Search the nooks and crannies of your image for specifics. Use your senses to give heft and texture to the details.

Of course, it is possible to use too many details, bogging down the forward motion of the story with details of the room where it takes place. Go ahead and put them in as they come to you in the first draft. As you rewrite, you'll trim, edit, and hone, keeping the strongest, the most telling details for the current piece and tossing the others, or storing them in the pantry of your notebook for another stew.

Naming people, places, and things is an effective use of detail that adds clarity and strength to your writing. When you name things, you are telling the truth. The Missouri River. The Sangre de Cristo Mountains. The chinook blowing in off the northwestern Pacific. Thursday. April. Whip-poor-will. Billy's Lunch Counter.

"Specificity is generosity," someone once said. Be a generous writer; give details as if they were gifts — from you to the reader.

{*See also* Pay Attention, p. 29; Guideline 9: Write Specific Details, p. 159}

THE WRITING LIFE

WRITERS ON READING

MICHAEL DORRIS wrote, "Reading anything that moves you, disturbs you, thrills you is a path into the great swirl of humanity, past, present, and future."

PHILIP ROTH reported that reading is a way to keep the circuits open and to think about the piece he's working on while getting a little rest from the actual work at hand.

> I've come to believe reading has as serious a relation to writing as do any number of activities such as staring pensively out the window or driving to Laramie.
>
> RICHARD HUGO

RAYMOND CARVER said he thought all writers — especially young writers — want to read anything they can get their hands on. He also said that finally, though, a young writer must choose between being a writer or a reader.

For **URSULA HEGI**, reading and rebellion were closely linked during her early teen years.

GRETEL EHRLICH said reading was an antidote for a "strongly felt cerebral loneliness." She described it as a passage out of the protective constraints prescribed for us by our parents and society.

Reading means questioning, said **J. D. McCLATCHY**, and "sensing that what you read is unfinished until it is completed in the self."

KATHLEEN NORRIS remarked that just the knowledge that a good book waited at the end of a long day made that day happier.

ROSE MACAULAY suggested there is only one hour in the day that is more pleasurable than the hour spent in bed with a book before going to sleep. It is "the hour spent in bed with a book after being called in the morning."

MARCH 16	Write about sinking
MARCH 17	An emergency exit
MARCH 18	Eating at a diner
MARCH 19	On the eve of the wedding
MARCH 20	Write about a family meal

KEEP THE WORLD ALIVE

Think of your favorite film. In it the actors speak their dialogue in voices that rise and fall, shout and whisper. We see their expressions, gestures, and movements, which "show" their emotions. For this story to take place somewhere, the director hired production designers and set decorators, prop masters who made sure the coffee cup was where it was supposed to be, the gun placed on the mantel. Costumers designed the clothes the actors wore. Lighting experts rendered the day bright or foggy, the room dim or candlelit.

> You need bits of the world to toss around. You start anywhere, and join the bits into a pattern by your writing about them.
>
> ⌐ ANNIE DILLARD ⌐

Sound mixers boomed out thunder or made a door creak. Music was composed, orchestras hired. After the film's closing scene, a string of credits numbering possibly into the hundreds named all the professionals who worked together to make the film.

Pity the writer, who must create all these elements by herself, with the only tool she has: language.

Writers in my group are used to seeing *keep the world alive* scribbled along the margins of their manuscripts. I, and the reader, want to know where we are; we need details of the physical setting to keep us grounded. We want to know what the weather's like. We want glimpses of the characters' faces and their bodies. We want to hear what they hear and to know how it sounds to them. We want to smell the roses and taste the whiskey and feel the air on their skin. We want to know, as E. L. Doctorow said, "not the fact that it is raining, but the feeling of being rained upon."

Keeping the world alive doesn't happen in the first draft. When you're flinging down the words to get the story out, you won't stop to bring in all these details. To do so is to risk losing all that heat you're generating on the page. Instead, you'll layer them in during your revisions, detail by concrete detail, honing the language and crafting the scene so that the story lifts off the page and the reader enters into the fictional world you've created.

FAVORITE WRITING TIPS

Oh, if I only knew what I was doing or *I wish there was a way to make this easier* or *if I knew what [fill in the blank] did to become a successful writer, then I could be one, too.* Seems we're all looking for tips to make our writing better, easier, more successful. How-to writing books abound, and we snatch them up and scour their pages. And you can bet, during most interviews with writers this question always comes around: what advice can you give to other writers? I asked the writers in my writing practice groups for their favorite bits of advice about writing, and they offered the following. Some of the quotations are from well-known writers, others from the group members themselves.

> I have distilled the rules and come up with one, just one, I feel can fit all of us: You should find what works best for you.
>
> ⌁ SUSAN POWER ⌁

"Keep your hand moving."
— Natalie Goldberg (from Kathy Allan, Judy Geraci, and others)

"You're free to write the worst junk in America."
— Natalie Goldberg (from Gina Cameron. Me, too.)

"Writing is as much discipline as it is desire."
— Christopher Bohjalian (from Jennifer Tuccillo)

"Don't spend time and money writing at coffee shops. You can brew your own coffee and don't have to go anywhere."
— Kristi Herrington

"Show, don't tell." — Bill Peters

"Write every day." — Refugio "Gio" Jones

"Write through your heart." — Chuck Hansen

"Write what you know."
— Mark Twain and others (from Rafael H. Gutierrez)

"Writing a novel is like driving a car at night. You can only see as far as your headlights, but you can make the whole trip that way."
— E. L. Doctorow (from Nicole Vollrath)

"Make your characters want something right away, even if it's only a glass of water." — Kurt Vonnegut (from Nicole Vollrath)

"Treat all your secondary characters like they think the book's about them." — Jocelyn Hughes

"I can't teach you to write. I can only help build your confidence." — Lewis Nordan (from Jay Katz)

And here are a few from my own Top Ten list:

"Don't think of words when you stop, but to see picture better." — Jack Kerouac

"Keep the world alive." — Janet Fitch

"Character lies in the destruction of the sentence." — Tom Spanbauer

MARCH 21	A single bed	
MARCH 22	The saxophone sound of midnight	
MARCH 23	Swimming against the tide	
MARCH 24	Write about an ending	
MARCH 25	"First time I saw her…"	

PRACTICAL USES FOR WRITING PRACTICE

All those hours scratching away in a mess of a notebook, all the bits and pieces, starts and stops, dead ends and U-turns. All those notebooks! How do I explain my writing practice to those who look askance at time spent scribbling what will most likely never lead to a finished product? And let's not even mention money. The idea of working without pay on something that is never intended to result in "return on investment" is not logical or rational behavior to those who aren't called to do it. Sometimes I wonder how I can even explain it to myself.

> Writing isn't about the destination — writing is the journey that transforms the soul and gives meaning to all else.
>
> ⌒ SUE GRAFTON ⌒

If what you need are some down-to-earth, feet-on-the-ground, practical uses and occasions for writing practice, here are a few:

- When you're between projects. Like a perpetual fountain (think chocolate or champagne), writing practice keeps the creative juices flowing.
- For writing outside the story. Writing practice gives you a place to explore aspects of your story or character that you won't actually use in the final piece but that will inform or shape what you're writing.
- To go deeper. Like writing outside the story, but many of these forays will be transferred to the story or piece, bringing added depth and meaning.
- When you're stuck on a project or just plain stuck. No pressure, no stress, just practice. Sometimes that's all you need to get back into the groove.
- As a daily centering/meditation/grounding practice. Like yoga for the creative spirit.
- For a friendly gathering of writing chums, if you're lucky enough to have a writing practice group.
- As a warm-up to revision or editing. Freewheeling practice opens creative connections.

- As a quickie to keep the writing muscles (heart and hand) in shape. A daily workout.
- To create flash fiction or flash memoir pieces. Sometimes all you need to produce these mini-pieces is the focus of a practice session, a good prompt, and the tension of timed writing.
- As building blocks for a longer piece (*see* Use Practice as Building Blocks, p. 126).

So the next time some practical-minded person lifts a skeptical eyebrow at the mention of writing practice, just offer up this list. Even, or maybe especially, if that person is you.

MARCH 26	Someone's playing the piano	
MARCH 27	You're taking off your clothes	
MARCH 28	Write the horizon at dusk	
MARCH 29	You ate it raw	
MARCH 30	In the backseat	
MARCH 31	The antidote to pain	

BEYOND PRACTICE

CAFÉ WRITING

Think of Paris. Henry Miller and Lawrence Durrell at La Coupole, Simone de Beauvoir and Jean-Paul Sartre at Café de Flore, Djuna Barnes and Saul Bellow at Café de la Mairie. Think of Ernest Hemingway at Les Deux Magots writing of a pretty girl "with a face as fresh as a newly minted coin if they minted coins in smooth flesh with rain-freshened skin."

Cafés have always presented writers a warm and friendly place for work and companionship. And not just in Paris. In San Francisco's Caffe Trieste, right around the corner from Lawrence Ferlinghetti's City Lights Bookstore, contingents of Beats gathered. And in *Writing Down the Bones*, you can follow Natalie Goldberg's trail in cafés from Taos to St. Paul.

Cafés offer writers ambience and aroma, conversation and coffee, often set against a background of good music you can listen to or not. The stimulation of sounds and smells and contained hubbub surfs the periphery of your senses while you lean into your notebook and write about somewhere else.

> A place belongs forever to whoever claims it hardest, remembers it most obsessively, wrenches it from itself, shapes it, renders it, loves it so radically that he remakes it.
>
> ⌒ JOAN DIDION ⌒

Morning, afternoon, evening — choose a time and take your notebook to your favorite café for a writing practice session. If you don't have a favorite place, make pilgrimages to several, finding one where you can settle in and make yourself comfortable. Plan to stay for an hour or an afternoon. Do timed writings, or let yourself write as long as you want. Write from a topic, then go back in and open the doors you have created (*see* Doors and Windows, p. 71).

Use your surroundings to add seasoning to your writing — bits of an overheard conversation here (that you eavesdrop on, oh so nonchalantly), a character sketch there (based on that very interesting man with the fedora who sits by the window reading Proust). Incorporate the art, the music, the light that transforms the glass bottles of flavoring into a shelf of decanted rainbows — fold all these café morsels into your writing like chocolate chips into cookie dough. Yum.

If you always go to the same café, just for a change try someplace new where the chairs aren't so familiar and the barista doesn't know your favorite drink. Change creates a tension that can inform your writing in subtle ways, just as does the very essence of the café.

Suggested prompts:

- Write about the taste of sorrow
- These are the things I saved
- Write about what is true at first light and a lie by noon (after Ernest Hemingway)
- "I stand between quiet and silence" (after Lizzie Wann)
- Write about a small rebellion
- Write about being in bad company

{APRIL}

*The imagination has resources and intimations
we don't even know about.*
— CYNTHIA OZICK

LET YOUR WRITING FIND
ITS OWN FORM

Form will come organically out of what you write. You don't have to have a beginning, middle, and end for what you write in practice sessions. In fact, if you are writing in short fifteen- or twenty-minute sessions, it will be difficult to create such a structure. Nor does what you write have to fit into some container labeled STORY or ESSAY or POEM. If you attempt to force form, you may miss revelations that might otherwise appear. Letting go of any preconceived ideas of what you want to write will set free a tremendous energy to write what wants to be written.

During any given practice session, you may write an essay, a poem, bits and pieces of a story, dialogue, fragments, a character sketch, or something more akin to a journal entry. Don't try to control your writing or make your writing into anything specific; just let it flow the way it wants. Like water following the path of least resistance, the real, authentic stuff will find its own way. Then, as you move through the exercise, a form will emerge. What begins as the cusp of a memory may evolve into a prose poem. A character sketch is suddenly a scene with two characters in dialogue, and one of them is pretty mad. A piece on what you learned in high school reads like the nub of a personal narrative. What a surprise when a 450-word flash fiction piece appears, and with just a little tweaking, you can turn it into something quite wonderful. Yet, if you'd tried for it, or anything specific, you might have missed the whole thing.

"One may do *anything*," Rilke told us. "This alone corresponds to the whole breadth life has."

TIP OF THE MONTH

Write something to suit yourself and many people will like it; write something to suit everybody and scarcely anyone will care for it.

— JESSE STUART

THE EFFECTS OF WRITING PRACTICE

If becoming a better writer were the only benefit of writing practice, it would be enough. But, as with so many other practices, what you get is often a whole lot more than you signed up for. Call them bonuses, rewards, extras, gifts, fringe benefits, or dividends, these are the promises inherent in writing practice.

- Daily writing practice sessions will improve your writing.
- Writing will come more easily and be less forced.
- You'll take more risks in your writing.
- You'll become less self-conscious; your writing will be looser, freer.
- You'll learn your rhythms as a writer, to trust your ups and downs.
- You'll find out what matters to you as a writer and what you want to write about.
- You'll discover your secrets and glimpse your shadows.
- You'll have an opportunity to grieve what needs to be grieved, and to heal.
- You'll feel good about yourself as writer and experience increased self-esteem.
- You'll explore clefts and chasms of stories and characters that will deepen a piece or open new worlds you might never have discovered otherwise.
- You'll fill notebooks, which may mean the beginnings, middles, and endings of some projects you didn't even know you wanted to write.

> Don't just plan to write — write. It is only by writing, not dreaming about it, that we develop our own style.
>
> ⌐ P. D. JAMES ⌐

The effects of daily writing practice may not come immediately, and they may be subtle in their appearance. But keep in mind there are those who believe the tiny flutter of a butterfly's wings in China creates hurricanes off the coast of Mexico.

{*See also* Practical Uses for Writing Practice, p. 59}

GO DEEPER

Sometimes a writer skates on top of a subject. Or tap-dances around it. The writing is glib and clever and absolutely without a trace of depth. Or maybe the writing is nice, like the sweet woman who wears pale flowered dresses and smiles no matter what. No one can find fault with her; it's just that she's so, well, nice. But somehow you don't quite trust her because you don't believe she's being honest. So it is when you hold back from a subject that has deeper meaning for you. You don't trust yourself, so you don't trust your writing.

> I'm constantly looking for things that are going to help me find the next sentence.
>
> ⌒ RON CARLSON ⌒

You may be able to write the facts of the subject: a father's death, a lover's parting, a fire, a flood, a terrible accident, childhood experiences related as if they happened to someone else. But you are afraid of the emotions that glide along on the underside of the facts like shadows beneath the ice.

If you are to write the truth, you must go beneath the surface into deeper, often darker waters where the light wavers and breathing is a matter of mindfulness.

"Often the writing process is filled with a sense of jeopardy," said Sue Grafton. Going to these deep and scary places takes courage. Kate Braverman told of a time she spent the night curled in the fetal position beneath her desk because of what she knew she must write, but she got up the next morning and continued writing. By writing the truth of your feelings, you get to feel them, and, once they're felt, you can begin to heal.

To go deeper in your writing:

- After you have written a certain passage that holds emotion for you, ask yourself how you feel. If you're writing fiction, ask how the character feels. Take a deep breath and experience the emotion in your body, then write what you felt. Never mind if you write clichés; you can always rewrite with fresher images. For now, just get it down.

- Instead of putting a period at the end of a sentence, put a comma and continue writing. Follow the last word with another specific image that takes the writing further, then do it again and again, with each image building to a more powerful effect. For example, from Evan S. Connell in "The Fisherman from Chihuahua": "His trousers, which were long and quite tight, concealed the fact that he was bowlegged, as befits certain types of men, and made one think of him easily riding a large fast horse, not necessarily toward a woman but in the direction of something more remote and mysterious." Using the comma rather than the period lets the words carry you deeper and deeper into the original image.

- If you stopped because you ran out of time, take more time. Or return to the piece in the next session and begin where you left off. Don't change the subject.

> I trust that help will come eventually if I persist in my curiosity, my investigation.
>
> ⮑ SUSAN POWER ⮐

- In rereading, if you notice a place where you pulled your punch, go back in and take off from just before the feint.
- Close your eyes and envision your face or your body, or that of the character you're writing. Write what you see.
- Write the sounds of the feeling. Or its colors. Feel the air that surrounds the emotion.
- Write through your tears. If you begin to cry, don't try to stop it, and don't stop writing, either. Let your tears fall on your page and smear your ink and mess up your writing. Remember what Robert Frost said: "No tears for the writer, no tears for the reader."

{*See also* Being Vulnerable on the Page, p. 123; Take Risks, p. 132; Breathe, p. 215; Slow Down, p. 85}

APRIL	1	Write about ordering in
APRIL	2	Write about a hot wind
APRIL	3	A stranger came to town
APRIL	4	Write about a summer fling (after k. d. lang)
APRIL	5	Something to be sorry for

PLACES TO PRACTICE

To say cafés may be redundant, but nevertheless, cafés top the list of favorite places to write. The ambience of sensory ambrosia plus the sweet quintessence of time set aside for good and important things make cafés and writing soul mates. But cafés aren't the only places I've put in some good writing practice time. Following is a list of locales I, and other writers, have practiced:

- **Laundromats:** Take all that mellow ambience of a café, turn it inside out with bright lights (probably fluorescent); gurgling, whooshing, thumping noises; the stink of dirty clothes, soap, and bleach; lint-filled air guaranteed to make you sneeze; time ticking away, quarter by quarter; and furrow-browed folks focused on mundane and necessary chores; and you've got the Laundromat. A completely different sensory experience and a stimulating place for writing practice. If you have to be there anyhow, what the heck, use it. Use it all.

> There is writing when you are intending to, and this other, less frequent, sometimes more beautiful writing that just comes.
>
> ⌒ JAMES SALTER ⌒

- **Outdoor areas in nature:** Parks and picnic areas and spaces that are green and lush and open to the sky make natural settings for writing. Sun shining or hidden by clouds, a little hot, too cool? Never mind. Take a walk, take your shoes off, take the time to lie back on the grass and write. And just because you're in the green and blue open spaces doesn't mean you have to write pastoral. Often the opposite of where we find ourselves is what we write, as Ernest Hemingway said, writing of Michigan while hunched over café au lait in a Parisian café.

- **Libraries and bookstores** (if they offer tables and chairs for lingering book lovers, as many do these days, complete with cafés): Who knows what thoughts or ideas or images or surprising and delicious phrases might find their way into your writing just by sharing the same literary aerie with all those books?

- **Bus depots, train stations, airports, and other way stations where travelers come and go:** Stay in one place and observe the people in transit. Pick up the buzz of motion and let its vibration inform your writing.

- **Public transportation:** Better still, get aboard that bus headed for the next town over, or hop an outbound train. Take the trolley to the end of the line, hail a taxi for a ten- or twenty-minute ride, or grab some other mode of public transportation. In our town we have romantic horse-and-carriages for hire, pedicabs peddled by sturdy young men with great smiles and muscled calves, short-run trams in all the tourist spots, and a harborful of water taxis, cruise boats, and ferries. You write while they drive, and let yourself be transported to somewhere else, both in body and writer's spirit.

- **Diners, lunch counters, delis, and coffee shops:** You may have to keep buying something to justify your counter space, but the milieu and its accompanying sounds, smells, and flavors can add as much spice to your writing as the Poupon. Never mind the corned beef stains. Leave a big tip.

> Live life and write about life.
>
> ⮜ WILL SELF ⮞

- **Bars, lounges, joints, and dives:** If it's not too dark and the music is good, go ahead. Use the sharp click-clack of pool balls, the hovering blue haze, and the beer breath of the place to accent your writing. But remember this: unlike genies, the Muse doesn't live in a bottle.

- **Your bed:** With pillows piled high behind you and maybe one on your lap to support your notebook, a steamy cup of hot coffee, mint tea, or cocoa within easy reach on the nightstand, where a candle dances and a sweet bouquet reminds you that you are loved (even if you bought it for yourself). Try this practice location first thing in the morning while sleep still clings to your consciousness, or at night before you slide down into dreamy repose. It's especially recommended in the midst of some rainy day just before or after you treat yourself to a lovely nap.

- **Your car:** Keep your notebook with you, and as you're going from here to there, and if it's a beautiful day, take a detour. Park at some fine lookout over a river or above the city or along a stretch of white-sand beach. Slide on over to the passenger side where you've got some elbow room, roll the window down, put your feet up, lean back, and write. Ah, that's better.

{
APRIL	**6**	It was a late night
APRIL	**7**	A candlelight vigil
APRIL	**8**	Write about small regrets
APRIL	**9**	Arriving on Saturday
APRIL	**10**	She lost all memory
}

DOORS AND WINDOWS

Each piece you write will have doors to open and windows to look through. As though you're exploring a house, let these openings reveal more of the place, what it's made of, how it's built, and the geography of the thing. Going through these doors and looking out these windows (or into them) provides the writer an opportunity for layering, creating texture and depth. When you reread your writing, make notes of these doors and windows. I draw little pictures on the page to remind me of where I sense an opportunity to go deeper. Later, in my rewriting, I enter them and follow their passageways and openings. Here are some examples of doors and windows that invite further exploration, sort of like an open house on an unhurried Sunday afternoon:

> There is a limited number of plots. There is no limit to the number of stories.
>
> ⌒ URSULA LeGUIN ⌒

- Let's say you're writing about a character who has dreams and fantasies. Rather than just ending the sentence in that vague place — "she had dreams at night" — open the door into the dreams and lay them out for the reader, like taking dresses out of the closet and spreading them across the bed.
- If being in a place reminds a character of her grandmother's house, go through that door and into a memory of the grandmother's house and something that happened there. The memory should not be random, however, but should relate somehow to what is happening to the character now.
- Describing that night twelve years ago as the most romantic night of your life is bland and meaningless until you pull back the blinds and bring the night into view with specific details of what made it romantic: the setting, the lighting, the way she leaned her head against your shoulder as you danced to "Begin the Beguine," the honeysuckle scent of her skin.
- If a character imagines the kind of woman her ex-lover is with now, describe that woman (bleached hair and long legs and shoes

with too many straps) and what the two of them might be doing together now (driving down the coast of California with its palm trees and frothing ocean, with the convertible top down and her hair blowing behind her like a flag of victory).

{*See also* Go Deeper, p. 66; Rereading Your Practice Pages, p. 185; Revising, p. 107}

	APRIL 11	Write about a place on a map
	APRIL 12	"After the final no…" (after Wallace Stevens)
	APRIL 13	Write about a passing sorrow
	APRIL 14	Write about "a history of whispers" (after Paul Simon)
	APRIL 15	On the edge of what felt safe

THE WRITING LIFE

WRITING POSITIONS AND CONDITIONS

Standers

Ernest Hemingway
Thomas Wolfe
Virginia Woolf
Lewis Carroll
Vladimir Nabokov

Lie-ers Down

Robert Louis Stevenson
Mark Twain
Truman Capote
Voltaire
Edith Sitwell (in an open coffin)

Bathtub Soakers

Benjamin Franklin
Edmond Rostand
Diane Ackerman

Writers in the Nude

Victor Hugo
Benjamin Franklin
D. H. Lawrence

Cigar Smokers

George Sand
Amy Lowell
Mark Twain (40 a day)

After a Long Walk–ers

Henry David Thoreau
Isaac Bashevis Singer (40–60 blocks
   every morning)
Wallace Stevens
Brenda Ueland
William Wordsworth
John Clare
Carl Sandburg (20 miles a day)
Charles Dickens (20–30 miles a day)

> Stay in your mental pyjamas all day.
>
> ⌐ COLM TOÍBÍN ⌐

WHEN YOUR WRITING BORES EVEN YOU

Boring writing happens when writers (a) get lazy, (b) keep treading the same old territory, (c) hold back, (d) play it too safe, or (e) get too comfortable. Here are some symptoms and antidotes.

A. Lazy Writing: The verbs graze on the hillside like fat cows, and the nouns are like cornmeal mush. The color palette is a six-pack of crayons, and the only textures mentioned are "soft" or "hard." The dialogue would make that of *Leave It to Beaver* sound clever. The writer has set new records for the number of clichés in one paragraph, and she ignores doors that might be opened and never looks out any windows.

Antidote: Play word games, experiment with language, audition words. Use the thesaurus, appropriate a set of paint chips from Home Depot and study the names of colors, take sensory inventories, practice writing dialogue, eavesdrop on conversations, read T. C. Boyle, Annie Dillard, Don DeLillo, Lorrie Moore. Reread your work and mark doors and windows. Open and enter them during writing practice exercises.

> Writing is a combination of ditch-digging, mountain-climbing, treadmill, and childbirth.
>
> ⁕ EDNA FERBER ⁕

B. Treading the Same Old Territory: Everybody in the group sighs when it's this writer's turn to read. We've all heard this story before. And before that and before that. As Herman's Hermits put it, in their classic song "I'm Henery the Eighth, I Am": "Second verse, same as the first" — it's another rewrite of the same interminable scene with only a few words changed, or it's another retread of the same story about the same characters singing the same tune. Boring!

Antidote: Freewrite using the writing practice prompts, writing only new material for the next month. No rewriting or editing allowed! Ban those characters from any further appearances in any stories from now on. Send them to the Retirement Home for Overused Characters. Flip everything: gender, age, profession, politics, hair color, diction, intelligence, geography, sexual preferences. Everything.

C. Holding Back: When vague words like *terrible*, *difficult*, and *painful* make regular appearances, or when clichés like *brokenhearted*, *sobbing like a child*, or *flew into a rage* are used to describe feelings, you can be fairly certain the writer is holding back. It's hard to care about people or characters who are held at arm's length by abstract words and hackneyed phrases. Readers want the real stuff: the truth.

> The discrepancy between what you ask for and what you get constitutes a story.
>
> ⌒ CHARLES BAXTER ⌒

Antidote: Ask what was it *exactly* that made something terrible. In what ways was it difficult? What did the pain feel like? Use concrete details and specific images. When a writer uses words like *terrible* or *difficult*, the reader has to go to her own image file to find something that is "terrible." She has to use her own judgment. Each time she has to do this, she's bumped out of the story. Use words that describe the terrible, difficult, painful. Show, don't tell. Write through the cliché with a fresh simile or metaphor. Ask what a broken heart feels like, looks like. Find fresh images. Go to your own experience, bring to mind a memory of a time you were brokenhearted, when you sobbed like a child, when you flew into a rage: describe your behavior and your feelings. Take the time to stay with the feeling and write down what you experience. Close your eyes and see the picture better. Write what you see.

D. Playing Safe: Safe writing is about as exciting as the seventh inning stretch at a bush-league ball game when the score is 13–0, visitor's favor. No wonder

APRIL 16	It's who you met at a party
APRIL 17	"Moving into the new house…"
APRIL 18	Write about black ice
APRIL 19	You're on a two-lane highway
APRIL 20	"Darkness comes at 3 in the afternoon" (after Robert Bly)

we're all yawning. Nothing's at stake here. So the cleanup batter hit a foul and broke his bat? Who cares. So their team's winning pitcher gets relieved by the kid up from the sagebrush league. Are we staying for the rest of the game, or are we going across the street for a beer?

Antidote: Write what matters. Be a passionate writer. We don't have enough time for our writing anyhow, so don't waste what little you have on something you don't care about. Also, for a reader to be involved in what she's reading, something must be at stake. There must be some kind of tension in the writing to keep the reader's attention. Crank up the heat, put some obstacles in the way of your characters. "Writing is not like parenting," said Romelda Shaffer. "Torment, confusion, obstacles, and catastrophes are good things."

When a writer is playing it safe, you can bet that the censor or critic is somewhere nearby.

> If you are not discouraged about your writing on a regular basis, you may not be trying hard enough.
>
> ⌐ MAXWELL PERKINS ⌐

E. Getting Too Comfortable: The writing is humming along. Show up at writing practice every day, same time, no problems. Writing is easy, four, five pages a day, meeting those goals. Found a genre that works, a groove that fits. Know how to play those plots and story lines, can write a poem on a dime; no surprises, no hassles. This writing business: easy pie.

Antidote: Just like the antidote for "playing safe," this writer needs to create some tension, turn up the burner, experience a little confusion. Change the time and place of the daily writing practice. Raise the bar to more pages every day. Switch genres; try something new. Don't fit so easily in the groove; feel the bumps and ridges, the sharp edge. Let your writing surprise you, keep you awake at night. If a writer is too comfortable, you can bet there aren't any risks being taken. No risks = boring writing.

"Beware of creating tedium!" said Anthony Trollope. "I know no guard against this so likely to be effective as the feeling of the writer himself. When once the sense that the thing is becoming long has grown upon him, he may be sure that it will grow upon his readers."

{*See also* Try Out Ideas, p. 88; Go Deeper, p. 66; Show, Don't Tell, p. 78; Better Verbs, Fewer Adverbs, p. 134}

SHOW, DON'T TELL

Here it is, that tired, threadbare piece of writing advice: show, don't tell. Thing is, it's valuable advice. Showing rather than telling is the best way for a writer to open wide the doors into the world she's creating and invite the reader in.

Here are a few ways to show rather than tell.

- Abstract words tell; concrete words show. Abstract words make the reader use her own judgment. Don't just say something is beautiful; show what beautiful is from the point of view of the one making the observation.
- Adjectives tell; verbs show. *She spoke in a high-pitched voice* vs. *She squeaked.*
- Generalizations tell; specificities show. *A house* or *a Spanish bungalow. A bird* or *a mourning dove. A flower* or *a gladiola.*
- Images create pictures; pictures show. Use language that calls up a physical sensation. "Louisiana in September was like an obscene phone call from nature." — Tom Robbins
- Write from the senses. We ground our writing in the concrete when we write through the senses, and it's through the senses that the reader enters the story. "You can't walk down a board sidewalk without clomping, so I clomped down to Ovcarik's Café and through the screen door, which banged shut as they always do." — William Least Heat-Moon

> Think big and stay particular.
>
> ⌒ ANDREW MOTION ⌒

- Show with description. Don't stop the movement of the story for description; make description part of the action. "A land turtle on the bank, startled, hissed the air from its lungs and withdrew into its shell." — Annie Dillard
- Show with character. The only way to have a clichéd character is by telling the general, rather than showing the specific. "He moves delicately, seeming to hover rather than stand: he has

about him the distant, omniscient, ectoplasmic air of the butler in a haunted house." — Larissa MacFarquhar

- Scenes bring the action close-up. Writing in scenes makes the story more immediate, more dramatic, and allows the reader to experience the events right along with the characters.

Of course, not everything can be "show, don't tell." We'd never get beyond the characters getting out of bed, brushing their teeth, eating breakfast, feeding the dog, and on and on, ad infinitum. You need narrative summary to span time ("Three weeks passed since..."), or to compress events ("Every Thanksgiving was the same until..."), or to give information ("And so ended the lesson on 'show, don't tell'").

> I had chanced upon the discovery that for the writer it is not moral pondering or grand emotion that are the entrance to a story, but detail and small event.
>
> ⟨ ETHAN CANIN ⟩

BEYOND PRACTICE

SPECIAL OCCASIONS

It's our nature as human beings to create ceremonies to mark special occasions. Whether we call them traditions, rites, rituals, observances, customs, or just "the way we do things," we perform acts in certain ways to honor an occasion or give a sense of occasion to an event.

We light candles on a birthday cake and sing "Happy Birthday," count down the seconds until the New Year, toast the bride and groom with champagne; every special occasion has its ceremonies. Even within our own families and groups, we honor rituals that mean nothing outside our circle. The plastic frog that somehow shows up in family pictures at every reunion. The picnic of fresh strawberries and shortcake every anniversary of meeting your partner.

Creating a ceremony and marking a special occasion with a writing session is a way for writers to express their feelings and reflections or memorialize the event in word pictures.

Light a candle and celebrate your birthday with a special writing session. Build a blazing solstice fire and record the midsummer night, or mark the winter solstice by writing your way through the longest night, sunset to sunrise. Gather flowers and surround yourself with sweet-smelling bouquets and honor the first day of spring by writing in your notebook, then pressing a flower between its pages.

> I think this is how we're supposed to be in the world — present and in awe.
>
> ⌐ ANNE LAMOTT ⌐

Every occasion can be made into ceremony if you give mindfulness to what the event means to you and what its larger meanings are. Your anniversary; a child's birth; the seasons, festivals, or celebrations of your faith; life passages; deaths.

The elements of ceremony include time set aside with a specific beginning and ending and a place that complements the event. Add elements such as music, candles, flowers or plants, special photographs, pictures or illustrations, significant tokens or symbols, or the wearing of special clothes or colors. Reading poems, prayers, or simply something you love may be included in the observance, too.

Ceremonies don't have to be complex or lengthy. Bring to the occasion that which is meaningful to you. And bring your notebook. When you are ready to write, simply begin with the time and place. "Summer Solstice, 2010. The Cove at La Jolla as the sun sets." Then, as with other writing sessions, simply follow your pen, one word and the next and the next.

This month's Beyond Practice offers topics rather than simple prompts for special occasion writing:

- Write remembrances of the occasion in times past
- Write the significance of the event at this particular time
- Describe and chronicle the elements of the ceremony
- Write a compilation since the last occasion (especially if you're writing your birthday or the New Year)

{MAY}

The role of the writer is not to say what all can say
but what we are unable to say.
— ANAÏS NIN

DON'T WORRY ABOUT THE RULES

It doesn't matter if your grammar is incorrect, your spelling wrong, your syntax garbled, or your punctuation off. Not during practice sessions, anyhow. Worrying about these rules during writing practice can trip up the intuitive flow of words and images. Pondering comma versus semicolon or whether *i* goes before *e* means you've crossed over that horizon from right brain to left brain to the place where there be dragons — the editor, judge, critic, and censor.

During practice sessions, if you can't spell a word, write it out as best you can; can't think of the name of a street or river or restaurant, draw a blank line that you fill in later. Find a shorthand that works for you, so long as you just keep moving forward, one word after the other. You can always go back, clean up, and correct if you want to use the practice piece in something else you're writing.

Having said all that, here's a word or two about the importance of correct spelling, grammar, and punctuation: Just as saws, hammers, screwdrivers, and awls are tools a carpenter needs, the basics of language usage are the tools of a writer's trade. As a writer, you should know how to use the language and be at ease with its rules. If your foundation is weak, shore it up. Get a good dictionary first of all, and books on basic English structure and usage. I like the classic *Elements of Style*, by William Strunk Jr. and E. B. White, and also *The Chicago Manual of Style*. These days, grammar and English usage books are a lot more fun than they ever let us know about in school: *Woe Is I*, by Patricia T. O'Conner; *Eats, Shoots & Leaves*, by Lynne Truss; *Sin and Syntax*, by Constance Hale; and a favorite of mine from a few years ago, *The Deluxe Transitive Vampire*, by Karen Elizabeth Gordon. Not to mention all the information available on the Internet. Got a question? Just type it in Google's search line, and you'll get pages and pages of answers to choose from. Maybe too many. You might also consider taking a course or getting a tutor. A final word of caution: You can trust the spelling checker on your computer only to a point — *bored* isn't the same thing as *board*, unless you happen to be at a long meeting around a corporate table, and putting your food in your mouth is much different from putting your foot in your mouth, though both can be hard to swallow.

TIP OF THE MONTH

Place is often something you don't see because you're so familiar with it.... But in fact it is the information your reader most wants to know.

— DOROTHY ALLISON

SLOW DOWN

Sometimes we're so anxious to get to the end of what we're writing that we go too fast, skipping over parts that cry out for closer inspection or that offer up a truth so simple we hardly recognize it.

It isn't only in writing that we go too fast, but in life as well. Maybe you think you have too much to do (which you probably have), so you feel an urgency to move through your list (and your life) as quickly as possible. You race out the door and down the steps without taking time to notice a fine curlicue of vine growing up the porch rail, or a couple of dogs chasing what could be a squirrel or merely a shadow.

> There is in every moment something that moves one intensely.
>
> ⌒ VINCENT VAN GOGH ⌒

The same is true with your writing; there are so many points to make, characters to get from here to there, that you zing from one to the next, a pebble across water, without taking the time to delve, to meander, to stay a while.

Before you begin writing, settle into your chair, feel the face of your page before you, the contours of your pen between your fingers. Breathe in and out a few times. Take your time and go slowly. Not so slow that you're sluggish and so is your writing; but slow as in peaceful, unhurried, at ease. When the pace of your writing picks up, follow it and keep its rhythm, but don't turn every corner, willy-nilly; don't cross the street until you've looked both ways.

When a door wants to be opened, open it, go inside, explore the room, sit on the sofa, plump the pillows, pull books from the bookshelf and page through them. Sniff the air and make note of the scents. If you feel uncomfortable in the room, all the more reason to stay and look around. It's often when the writing gets uncomfortable that we want to hurry along. Don't. Loosen the grip on your pen, stay in the room, and breathe.

MAY 1	This is what I remember
MAY 2	Mother said
MAY 3	First time we met
MAY 4	She (he) rode off on a Harley
MAY 5	The moon made me do it

TOP TEN EXCUSES NOT TO PRACTICE...

In his book *The Lie That Tells the Truth*, John Dufresne writes, "Excuses — we've got a million of them. In the writing world, however, excuses are irrelevant." Nonetheless, when asked, a bevy of writing practice experts offered up these top ten excuses not to practice.

1. Cleaning, laundry, shopping, lawn to mow; too busy, too many chores.
2. Not enough time. "Can't write my novel tonight, so why start?" "I'll just get started, then it'll be time to quit, so why even start?"
3. Others (spouse, children, family, pets) need me.
4. I'm too tired.
5. I'm not inspired now, but I will be later. I can't focus, don't feel creative, have to get in the mood.
6. Need to exercise.
7. Nap time, bedtime.
8. My characters aren't talking to me. I'm stuck on plot, need to do more research, need to make more notes.
9. I have nothing good to write, nothing to say. I cannot write.
10. I'd rather read (it will inspire me) or watch TV or play on the Internet.

> Turn up for work. Discipline allows creative freedom. No discipline equals no freedom.
>
> ⌒ JEANETTE WINTERSON ⌒

And, of course, the moon is full, there is no moon, Mercury is in retrograde, the Cubs lost, I'm having my period, we're out of coffee.

MAY 6	Rain, heavy on the windows...
MAY 7	Write about the opening of blossoms
MAY 8	What made you laugh
MAY 9	A green-eyed woman
MAY 10	Write about a sudden silence

...AND WHAT TO DO ABOUT THEM

Excuses not to write are just that. Excuses. Here's how to overcome them:

- Make a date with yourself for a practice session, set aside that time in your daily schedule, write it in your calendar (in ink), and honor it. If you use an electronic calendar, set it with a special tone to remind you when it's practice time.

- If you miss the session, write in your calendar the reason you didn't show up. List what you did instead. These notes can give you insight into what a therapist might term your "avoidance behavior." But we'll just label them EXCUSES.

- Make a date with a writing friend. For some reason, we tend not to break dates with our friends as easily as we break them with ourselves. (How to be your own best writing friend? Show up when you say you will.)

- Start a writing practice group — with regular attendance as a prerequisite for membership.

- Reward yourself for practice time put in. (You'll soon find that the rewards are inherent in the doing.)

> Every morning or afternoon, whenever you want to write, you have to go up and shoot that old bear under your desk between the eyes.
>
> ⮌ ROBERT LECKIE ⮎

- If you succumbed to an excuse today, own up to the fact that you're using excuses to not write (what's that all about?), then start again tomorrow by making an appointment with your writing self.

- Write a letter to yourself expressing why taking the time for writing practice is important, and write as if you were talking to your very best friend. Say how you see yourself as a writer and what writing means to you. Just for fun, self-address and stamp the letter and give it to a friend to mail to you sometime in the future without telling you when to expect it.

{*See also* Daily Routine, p. 21; The Discipline of Writing, p. 195}

TRY OUT IDEAS

No place is safer for trying out ideas — even the most radical — than your writing practice notebook. You've got time and all the pages you need. You've even got permission to write badly and to stop any time you want. So go ahead, take that hub of an idea out for a spin. See what happens.

- Want to try writing Elmore Leonard–style dialogue — cool and spare and uncannily natural? Go ahead. Or give inanimate objects a voice: let carrots talk to peas, motorcycles talk to cars, photographs talk to subjects.
- Never tried your hand at genre writing? Create a fantasy, a western, sci-fi. Or even the bodice-ripping, heavy-breathing purple prose of an old-fashioned romance. Who's to read this stuff unless you invite them?
- Write erotica. Not that bodice-ripping, old-fashioned purple prose, but the real stuff. The Anne Rice as Anne Rampling, the Susie Bright, the *Yellow Silk* or *Black Lace* of erotica.
- Have an idea and don't know whether it fits fiction, play, or screenplay? Try some of each.
- Never written a screenplay? Go for it, a few pages worth, in your notebook. On a Saturday afternoon. Look through the camera of your mind.
- Change point of view; write the story from one character's point of view, then try another. Go from first person to third. Past to present tense.
- If you're stuck at a juncture of a story and don't know which road to take, travel a little ways down all of them; notice the scenery, the weather, the possible destination.
- Ask the perennial question of fiction writers everywhere, "What if...?" Ask it even if you're not writing fiction.

Writers aren't born knowing the craft; writers are born with an urge to write, a curiosity, an imagination, and, perhaps, a love of the language. The way to learn the craft is through practice, and your notebook is the place of your apprenticeship. Even writers who are expert in the craft (those who've practiced long and hard) still try out ideas.

{*See also* When Your Writing Bores Even You, p. 74; Gifts from the Muse: Phrases, Images, and Other Kindnesses, p. 133; Hunting and Gathering, p. 152}

> The sensation of writing a book is the sensation of spinning, blinded by love and daring.
>
> ANNIE DILLARD

HOW TO TELL WHEN THE CRITIC IS PRESENT...AND WHAT TO DO ABOUT IT

Here's a list of telltale signs that the critic is sitting, if not on your shoulder, at least in the room somewhere.

- You stop writing in the middle of a piece and say something like "This is not working" or worse, "This is crap" or "This sucks."
- You hear voices demanding, "Who do you think you are?" or "You call that writing?" or "You think anybody will ever buy that? Fool." Thin, tinfoil voices that sound as if they're passing through pinched lips and tight mouths.
- You can't write what you want to write; your writing dead-ends or trails off into drivel.
- Your pen is afraid to touch the paper, almost as if there's some invisible block between pen and page.

> Love your material. Nothing frightens the inner critic more than a writer who loves her work.
>
> ⌒ ALLEGRA GOODMAN ⌒

- You stop writing on the topic and instead write unkind notes to yourself: "This is junk" or "Blah, blah, blah" or other, more critical comments.
- You start to judge even your handwriting, saying how bad it is, how sloppy, that no one could possibly read it.
- You judge your hands, how scruffy and unkempt your nails are, how the pen you've chosen is all wrong.
- You channel people who've criticized your writing, or images of them appear on your page; they're usually smirking. A whole gallery of smirking faces, or that one single idiot with a pea-sized brain and bad breath who told you to consider your day job as a career path.
- You imagine people laughing behind your back, not just agents or editors but your close friends, who all agree your writing is so bad it's hilarious.

This nasty con artist of a voice is your own self-doubt and negativity, and it must be silenced if you are to get any work done.

You can trash the critic. Draw pictures of its ugly face, then tear them into tiny pieces and toss them in the garbage. Or set them ablaze.

You can write all the lines that voice feeds you on strips of paper and put them in a jar. Close the jar tightly so no air can get in and stash it on a shelf deep in your pantry where the light can't reach it. Or in the back of your closet beneath all those old shoes. Maybe in the furthest reaches of the garage. Or the basement. Leave it to the roaches and spiders.

> You get your confidence and intuition back by trusting yourself, by being militantly on your side.
>
> ⌐ ANNE LAMOTT ⌐

You can make a deal with the critic. Ask it to wait outside until you've finished your work, then you'll give it voice (which is a lie, but who's to know).

You can scare the little bully off by outbullying it: "Get out of here, you twerp!"

You can ignore it, give it the old silent treatment until it finally gets bored and skulks away. (Note: this can take more time than you have.)

You can recognize it for what it is, self-doubt and fear; acknowledge it; then get on with your writing. Take heart that you're not alone. All writers, at some time or other, wilt under the hot breath of the Critic. But if you keep writing no matter what, chances are you can bypass this dead-end road and keep heading west, into the sunset.

MAY 16	Awake at first light
MAY 17	It's in the cards
MAY 18	Write about a picnic
MAY 19	What waits at the top of the stairs
MAY 20	Write about a painting

TURN THE SOIL

Think of a garden and the rich, loamy earth that's exposed when you heave to with hoe and spade. This is what happens when you practice. When you write about that summer day when the sun was heavy in the sky and you and your father were fishing on the banks of the Platte River, his red-and-white plastic bobber bouncing on the milk chocolate water — you are turning the soil of memory with your spade of a pen. Breathe in and smell its fecund possibilities; get down on your hands and knees for a close-up of the living things you've unearthed.

You keep writing, turning the soil, going deeper, mixing it up. Surprised, maybe, at what you've excavated and curious — why this image, this day?

One day's session may take you into a memory of rafting down the Colorado River through the vast split of the Grand Canyon. You try to go back to it the next day but instead find yourself describing the lopsided grin of the waitress who served you hash and eggs at breakfast that morning. Not until two weeks later do you write about the canyon again; you and your husband stretched out next to each other in your sleeping bags, watching the moon volley the tall walls above you. You keep writing and you unearth more — the icy clamp of the water when you tried to rinse shampoo from your hair; him fishing at the edge of the river, whistling as he always did when he fished. But next day's practice, it's something else — the smell of wild lilac on the hillside that leads you into your grandmother's bedroom. Like Brigadoon, the Grand Canyon is lost to you again.

Just as new sprouts take their time breaking through the earth, you can't demand an image to appear. Instead, you hoe, you shovel, you take off your shirt and bend to your weeding. Then, one day, you're writing about a street you once lived on and, without willing, the memory of that last trip to the Grand Canyon comes. This time the images arrive at full tilt: the echo inside the wide mouth of a rock cave when he said your name, the auburn glint of his hair as he shaded the sun from your face and made promises he wouldn't be able to keep of returning to this place. The words you write are

> Writing is an exploration. You start from nothing and learn as you go.
>
> ⌒ E. L. DOCTOROW ⌒

true, and you are able, this time, to write into the memory through your pain and your tears.

Think of each practice session as an exercise in gardening. After only one or two weeks of writing, you won't have rows of corn, all silk tasseled and ripe for harvest. You may have a single row of soil half-turned, where later you'll drop seeds, one by one, and maybe, if the weather holds and the alchemy is right, within a few more weeks tiny green seedlings might break through. Not all your seeds will sprout, however, and the harvest won't come this month, or even the next. It takes time to grow a garden; it takes time to write what wants to be written. Rainer Maria Rilke reminded us to "always wish that you may find patience enough in yourself to endure, and simplicity enough to believe."

> I use my fiction to explore my own unconscious issues. I usually don't even know what's going on with me until I'm writing.
>
> ⌁ JANET FITCH ⌁

THE WRITING LIFE

WHEN THEY BECAME WRITERS

M. F. K. FISHER said she became a writer when she was four. It was her way of screaming and yelling, the primal scream.

MADELEINE L'ENGLE knew she was going to be a writer from the moment she wrote her first story. "I was five and it was called 'G-R-U-L.' I didn't know how to spell girl. My father got a new typewriter when I was ten and gave me his old one. I immediately wrote my first novel."

JAMES MICHENER didn't start writing until he was forty. Stationed on an island from 1944 through 1946, he wrote *Tales of the South Pacific*, the first writing he had done. After he completed it, he decided to become a writer.

ANNE LAMOTT said, "All of a sudden [during the writing of *Hard Laughter*] there was some structure and there was some order and there was a point A where the book begins and a point B where the book ends. I became a writer."

MAY SARTON was "reborn" as a writer at age twenty-six after a failure in the theater.

JAY McINERNEY claimed writing was something he wanted to do since he could remember, aside from a brief notion of being a trapper in the Hudson Bay, or a mercenary.

AGATHA CHRISTIE, previously a poet and writer of children's books, began writing detective mysteries at age thirty after being challenged by her sister who said she could not handle the rules governing that genre. She wrote thirty Poirot books.

> I was gravely warned by some of my female acquaintances that no woman could expect to be regarded as a lady after she had written a book.
>
> ⌘ LYDIA MARIA CHILD ⌘

AMY TAN decided to do something for herself when her friends called her a workaholic. "I at first went to a psychiatrist about this, but after he fell asleep three times during sessions, I decided I would try my own kind of therapy, so I studied jazz piano and tried to write something that I really wanted to write."

MARGE PIERCY said she became a writer at fifteen, when her parents moved into a house where she had a room of her own and a door that shut.

EUGÈNE IONESCO claimed he was always a writer. "I wanted to write my memoirs at ten."

MARGARET ATWOOD was crossing the football field on the way home from school when she wrote a poem in her head. "Then I wrote it down, and after that, writing was the only thing I wanted to do."

ALICE McDERMOTT's sophomore college writing professor called her into his office and said, "I've got bad news for you. You're a writer and you're never going to shake it."

> It's easy, after all, not to be a writer. Most people aren't writers, and very little harm comes to them.
>
> ⌁ JULIAN BARNES ⌁

RAYMOND CARVER was in college, too, an undergraduate at Humboldt State. "One day I had a short story taken at one magazine and a poem taken at another. It was a terrific day! Maybe one of the best days ever."

When she was seven, **DOROTHY WEST** asked her mother if she could close her door. Her mother said yes and asked why. "Because I want to think." When Dorothy was eleven, she asked her mother if she could lock her door. Her mother said yes and asked why. She said, "Because I want to write."

JOSEPH WAMBAUGH first became aware of himself as a writer with the completion of his third book.

LYNN SHARON SCHWARTZ said, "It's impossible to be a 'good girl' and a writer at the same time. When I was about thirty-two, it dawned on me I had to make a choice: 'be good' or be a writer. And I decided to be a writer."

And you?

WRITING MEMORY

Our memories are shape-shifters. The moment an event or experience or an image is observed and clicked into place in memory, it is already fiction. It has taken a different form in that moment, and it will take a different form again when we retrieve it, or when, as if by the striking of some sensory gong, it surfaces unbidden. These are some of the ways memory fictionalizes events:

1. Everything is altered by our perceptions even as it is lodged into memory.

    Try this exercise: Write an event in your notebook, something that happened recently. In three weeks or a month, without rereading your original entry, write the same event again. Compare the two to see how your memory has reshaped certain details and which details surface in the second telling. It's possible you'll remember some aspects you didn't note in the first recording — some, in fact, you didn't even know you noticed at the time of the event.

> Every man's memory is his private literature.
>
> ⌒ ALDOUS HUXLEY ⌒

2. Our emotional states alter our memories. How we feel at the time of an experience or event informs the way we remember it. Then, when we recall the event, the emotional state we're in at that time reshapes the memory once more. An example: how we remember our wedding in the days and weeks right after it, and how we recollect it some years later, after the divorce.

3. Changing situations alter memories. Certain events or times in our lives may become shaded with a rosy light when we are no longer experiencing them. This is how our words become tinged with nostalgia when we write of the good old days. "It was one of those perfect English autumnal days which occur more frequently in memory than in life," wrote P. D. James.

4. Just as things are altered by our perceptions as they are lodged into memory, our changing perceptions of ourselves change our memories; the stories memory holds are reshaped by the voice of the reminiscent narrator. The memories we write are hedged

with a certain tone or attitude as they unreel on the page. Memoirists, especially, will recognize this phenomenon.

5. Time alters memory. We lose details or confuse facts after a length of time. And not just because we age. Isn't it amazing how we can recall the exact pair of earrings we were wearing when we caught a glimpse of George Clooney eating melon with prosciutto at that little trattoria on Lake Como, but we can't remember if it was on our first or our third trip to Italy?

6. So too, people, places, and events run together in our memory. This is called the fuzzing factor and is one good argument for keeping a journal. Especially if you plan to write memoir.

> Sometimes, for me, writing is about making conscious what I already know.
>
> ⟜ ABHA DAWESAR ⟞

7. We alter the memory as we retell the story to different people. Depending on the response we want from the listener, or the effect we want the story to have, we relate certain details and leave out others, or we put emphasis on particular aspects of an event and de-emphasize others. Politicians and image-makers call this "spin." For writers, it's good storytelling.

8. We add to memory to make sense of what happened. The stories we create from real life are often written as a way of deepening our understanding of an experience. Sometimes these made-up stories become part of the memory itself. Did my father really fire a gun into the air to see if it worked, or did I make that up? Did he even have a gun the day he and Uncle Bob went out to find the man who molested my sister? I swear I don't recall.

MAY 26	She said a prayer
MAY 27	Nothing can be heard
MAY 28	"That night I was happy"
MAY 29	The color of midnight
MAY 30	Write the first time
MAY 31	A red car

AVOIDING THE TRUTH

One way or another, writing brings us to our truth, which is not always the destination for which we bought a ticket. The truth can feel dangerous — as if you're exposing yourself or telling secrets. Sometimes, without even knowing it, we avoid, sidestep, bypass, or otherwise circumnavigate the truth in our writing. Here are some checkpoints to look for in your writing that indicate you might be avoiding the truth:

- Changing the subject
- Nattering on and on about meaningless details
- Closing up
- Becoming glib
- Being nice
- Using generalities instead of specifics
- Hurrying along
- Looking the other way
- Ignoring the naked emperor riding by and the elephant in the living room
- Glossing over the top, like a coat of wax.
- Affecting attitude; posing
- Tap-dancing around the topic
- Killing the messenger (getting rid of a character, one way or another)
- Filling the stage (bringing in a host of characters to distract, like company)
- Leaving the scene (someone exits)
- Bringing in *outside forces* (suddenly, the phone rang; someone knocked; lightning struck)
- Abandoning the piece
- Starting something entirely new, on a different topic
- Not writing

> I'm usually afraid of what I really want to write....When I aim at the far, when I'm brave, I find it liberating, and the best material comes from it.
>
> — SIRI HUSTVEDT

These avoidances in writing are just like avoidances in real life except perhaps more obvious and lasting because they're in black and white. Writing the truth is always a challenge to the writer. This is what Willa Cather said: "Artistic growth is, more than it is anything else, a refining of the sense of truthfulness. The stupid believe that to be truthful is easy; only the artist, the great artist, knows how difficult it is."

{*See also* Take Risks, p. 132; How to Tell When the Censor Is Present, p. 175; Tell Your Secrets, p. 212}

> While writing — that's when I face the exposure....That's when I always have to bear down and try to write as closely to what is the truth as I can feel it with my senses and with my heart.
>
> ⟬ ANDRE DUBUS ⟭

BEYOND PRACTICE

"...IN WANDERING MAZES, LOST"

This line, borrowed from John Milton, invites you to wander, meander, lose your bearings — not in "elevated thought," as the poet wrote, but in place. Not so lost that they have to send out the dogs, but lost enough that you are uncertain of exactly where you are or how to find your way home again.

With notebook in hand, wander neighborhoods you're unfamiliar with, a part of town you don't know. Or drive to another community. Better yet, take the train or a bus. Travel a different road, turn this way and that until you're not quite sure where you are and don't recognize the landmarks. Or walk a well-known trail, then veer off in a direction you've not gone before, where you don't know what to expect. In town or out, get off the beaten path and venture into the wilds.

This special writing practice session suggests that the effects of unfamiliar territory and the tension of not knowing exactly where you are or how to get home can be good for your writing. And your soul. Most likely you'll pay more attention to the details of the place, notice the specifics: the names of streets and shops, the architecture and geography, flora and fauna. Being lost, your senses will be on the alert; you may have your psychic guard up, too, and feel somewhat wary of strangers. You're in foreign territory and they're the natives.

Allow a generous amount of time for this special session. Who knows how long it might take to find your way home again. You may discover one place that invites a writing, and then, after you've completed a session and continue on your way, another location will call out to you and you'll just have to write again. Give yourself over to the adventure. Make generous notes in your notebook about the feelings and sensations of being lost.

This is another Beyond Practice session that's better done alone. Taking a pal along removes

> If a man does not keep pace with his companions, perhaps it is because he hears a different drummer. Let him step to the music which he hears, however measured or far away.
>
> ⟜ HENRY DAVID THOREAU ⟞

some of the tension from that delicious scary feeling of being lost and creates a safety and distraction that is at odds with the intention of the exercise.

Take maps if you must. Turn off your cell phone. (Imagine leaving home without it.) If you do venture into the wilds, prepare yourself with provisions. This exercise isn't suggesting you put yourself in any real danger. Just create some suspense, heighten your awareness, titillate your senses.

Here are some prompts for the adventure, or create your own from the environment and your sensations, both inner and outer.

- Write about a time of small despair
- Write about being on the outside
- "Death changes everything" (after Dorothy Allison)
- Write about a spiderweb
- "My real name is . . ."

{ JUNE }

You're a Genius all the time.
— JACK KEROUAC

LET GO OF EXPECTATIONS

Expectations set you up so you're always ahead of yourself rather than being present in the moment. This is why it's good to dive right into the writing prompt with no time to think of what you'll write or how best to shape your writing around the subject.

For example, let's say something important has happened in your life and you believe you should write about it. You give a cursory look at the day's prompt, then try to bend it around what you want to write about. Instead of the writing flowing freely, you can't get a word out, or if you do, it's a puny, shriveled little word, inadequate for the important subject you tried to write about.

Another example: You're feeling lethargic, low energy, and definitely not creative. But you've committed to a practice session and, good for you, you're going to show up at the page, no matter what. You arrive grudgingly and a little resentful, muttering under your breath, "Okay, I'll go, but I won't write anything good." And, of course, you don't. In this case, unfortunately your expectations have been fulfilled.

Zen master Hakiun wrote, "If you forget yourself, you become the universe." How do you let go of expectations? Before you begin writing, take a few moments to clear your mind. Settle into your place and breathe deeply in and out a few times. Let your mind be open and peaceful before you begin, and let your writing surprise you. One of the comments most often repeated at writing practice groups is "I don't know where that came from." It's usually said with some amazement.

TIP OF THE MONTH

Compose with utter freedom and edit with utter discipline.

— ERICA JONG

JUNE 1	In the back of the closet
JUNE 2	Alone in her room
JUNE 3	"He refuses all fear" (after Pierre Reverdy)
JUNE 4	You don't know where you are
JUNE 5	Write about a black dress

HOW CAN I TELL IF MY WRITING IS IMPROVING?

A promise inherent in the concept of writing practice, or for that fact, the steady practice of anything — glassblowing, layups, a foreign language, hanging wallpaper — is that the more you practice, the better you'll get. Unfortunately, we're not always the best judge of our own work; sometimes we're too close to notice any improvements. Or the critic's voice is louder than any other voice, so we always hear what's wrong with our writing, not what's good or what's getting better.

> Eventually the craft becomes second nature, and the work becomes stronger for your having learned it.
>
> ⌒ JULIE ORRINGER ⌒

You may recognize that your writing is becoming freer, more facile. You may find yourself liking more of what you've written, and perhaps you do sense a general improvement. However, if you want a more specific yardstick, you can use the following checklist to measure your writing progress.

- ❑ You easily fall into writing from the prompt and begin writing without hesitation; you don't stop to think or consider; you just keep the pen moving.
- ❑ You stay with the image or memory engendered by the prompt long enough to explore it, rather than verging off into digressions that go nowhere or jumping from one thought to the next. You are a more patient writer.
- ❑ You stay out of journal writing and in creative writing mode; you keep yourself out of the way.
- ❑ Your verbs are lively and diverse.
- ❑ Your images are fresh.
- ❑ You write with fewer clichéd words and images.
- ❑ Your sentences vary in length and structure.
- ❑ Instead of putting a period at the end of a sentence, you put a comma and take the thought further.
- ❑ You write more naturally, with less self-consciousness.
- ❑ Adverbs have all but disappeared from your writing.

- ❑ Your writing is truthful and honest. You don't hold back.
- ❑ Ah, those details you have chosen. Delicious.
- ❑ You layer your writing with sensory images. You include smells, sounds, and textures as well as visuals. You let sensory images do double duty for you, crafting tasted emotions, heard colors, colored sounds. Your words create moods.
- ❑ You don't overwrite, nor are you stingy with words.
- ❑ You have expanded your language, learned new words.
- ❑ You write in the active voice.
- ❑ You save the strongest word for the last in the sentence, without the sentence sounding forced.
- ❑ You don't rush through to get to the end but take your time, lingering and savoring. Letting the tension build.
- ❑ You take more risks.
- ❑ You don't pull your punches.
- ❑ You've eliminated generalities; you write in specifics.
- ❑ You're willing to experiment, to try out, to go to unknown places in your writing.

As for the idea that "practice makes perfect," it's a lie. There is no perfect, only better and sometimes, very, very good.

{
JUNE 6	While the world sleeps	
JUNE 7	I have a confession to make	
JUNE 8	"There is a place somewhere called Paris" (after César Vallejo)	
JUNE 9	Across the railroad tracks	
JUNE 10	The place where wild pines grow	
}

REVISING

There's a reason they call them drafts and give them numbers like first, second, third, and so on, sometimes up into the thirties or forties before they are pronounced *final drafts*. This reason is revision, and some say it's the best part of writing. Bernard Malamud, for example, called revising "one of the exquisite pleasures of writing."

Writing is a two-step process. First, getting down the raw, uncut first draft, which has a right to be messy, unordered, disconnected, and rambling. After all, the writer is following the path beaten out by intuition, and intuition sets a lively pace that doesn't allow for stopping to get your bearings.

The second step is revising. This is where the writer cuts and hacks away, reordering and rearranging, rewriting to discover more of what the piece wants to be. This revising will send you back to the first draft again as you find doors to go through and holes to fill, and you'll continue the process of writing, rewriting, writing, rewriting. For most writers, the second step takes longer. "I tacitly assume that the first fifty ways I try it are going to be wrong," said James Dickey. A few cautionary thoughts:

> Half my life is an act of revision.
>
> ⌒ JOHN IRVING ⌒

- Too much rewriting can tame the wildness right out of your work, leaving a piece of writing that's as flat as the path you've trodden to get there.

- No matter how massive your computer's memory, the machine is only as reliable as your last save command. Use external backups and drives, too. Some advise keeping a backup in a remote location, just in case. Make a copy of every draft. You may like an idea you had in the second draft better than what you wrote in the seventh.

- Revising before you've reached the end of the first draft may keep you from ever finishing a piece. As novelist Pearl S. Buck put it, "You're likely to begin dawdling with the revisions and putting off the difficult task of writing."

SAYING NO TO THE MUSE

Let's say you're in the midst of a writing session, chugging along at a good rate, maybe you're arm wrestling it some, trying to get where you know you want to go. Suddenly you feel a buzzing little whisper that tickles your ear or a slight tugging at your psychic sleeve. Instead of tuning in for a minute to see what might want your attention, you brush it off; you keep trudging forward, certain that the direction you're going in is the only road home.

> Not writing is probably the most exhausting profession I've ever encountered. It's very psychically wearing not to write — I mean if you're supposed to be writing.
>
> ⌐ FRAN LEBOWITZ ⌐

Or let's say you do take notice of that quick flash of thought or niggling little idea, but with hardly more than a sideways glance, you dismiss it like royalty ignoring a servant. Whether you say these exact words aloud or not, when thoughts like the following cross your mind, you're saying no to the Muse.

- My character wouldn't do that.
- That's stupid!
- I can't possibly write *that*.
- How does that fit in with what I'm writing?
- I need more time to think about that.
- You're getting in the way of what I'm doing here.
- I don't have the energy right now to follow you.
- You're scaring me.
- I don't understand what you want me to write.
- Just let me do this first.
- That's not logical.
- That's boring. No one is interested in that.
- That could never happen.
- Ah, that feels a little too painful. Maybe later.
- Help me with what I'm doing here, and we'll get back to your idea.
- That's cute, but it wouldn't work here.

- Too far out. Nobody would believe it.
- Can you come back tomorrow?

Though she has the patience of a saint, the Muse doesn't like to be ignored. If you don't pay attention, she may stop paying calls.

SAYING YES TO THE MUSE

The Muse doesn't keep a time schedule. She may ignore your requests for her presence and then show up when you least expect her and when it's most inconvenient. She does not honor demands. Rather, she likes to be coaxed, prepared for, made welcome. And then, some wondrous, surprising times, she simply appears. Like a gift, or grace.

> Literature...thrives on an abandonment of repression, a willingness to say anything, espouse, describe, and suggest anything at all.
>
> ⁕ SCOTT SPENCER ⁕

As a writer or any artist, it's important to always welcome her, to accept her favors and presence. If you shun her, she's likely to find you an unreliable host and withhold her visits. Say yes to the Muse by doing the following:

- Keep pen and paper always nearby to write down those lines and ideas and thoughts — in your car, beside your bed, with you as you go for walks, work in the garden, do the dishes.
- Make use of the note-taking tools on your mobile devices or Stickies on your computer.
- Honor the gift by writing it down as it comes; get out of the shower, pull off to the side of the road, excuse yourself from a conversation. As with a dream, you may believe you'll remember, but these visitations are tenuous, gossamer threads of imagination or intuition that disappear like morning mist into sunlight.
- Leave an open space in your mind. Try to not always be thinking, planning, evaluating. Breathe in and out and let your mind be at rest, open and welcoming to gentle, unplanned thoughts and ideas.
- Set a place for the Muse with lovely things: candles and flowers, music and art, colors, textures, scents, things you love that have meaning for you.
- Be present at an appointed time. Some say that if you show up at the same place and the same time every day, your creative self will know it's time to go to work. The Muse will know where and when to find you.

THE WARP AND WOOF
OF WRITING PRACTICE

Filling your practice notebook, you'll produce story shoots, the beginnings (or middles) of essays, fragments of memoir or personal narrative, monologues, characters who want you to write them, maybe even a few pages of a play or screenplay. Your notebooks will show you not only what you want to write about but also the genre it wants to take.

You can continue to develop these beginnings in two ways: (1) transfer the rough drafts to your computer or word processor and work on editing and revising, and (2) continue to work in your practice sessions on other sections of the piece, letting the fresh material spill into your notebook.

In time, there comes a rhythm of movement between the spontaneous stuff of writing practice and the thoughtful work of editing, revising, and rewriting. An in-and-out process of creating, then revising — dropping down into the intuitive, unrestrained place of origination, then coming up to the more deliberate setting of choice and measured consideration.

Some writers like to work weeks or even longer on the raw material, even to what feels like the completion of a first draft. Others write in their notebook for a time every day, then by that evening have it transferred to computer to read over and edit. Or they may begin the next day with the edits before they move back into their notebook. There's no right or wrong way to do it; each writer has to discover his or her own way. This is another of the freedoms and responsibilities of art. There are many great teachers, but no one can say "This is the way you *must* do it"; they can only say "This is the way I do it."

> We work in the dark — we do what we can — we give what we have. Our doubt is our passion and our passion is our task. The rest is the madness of art.
>
> ⮞ HENRY JAMES ⮜

You will come to know your own rhythms — when you have been traveling the heady path of creation and sense it's time to transfer the piece into a construct of some sort, and when you need to move back again from the cerebral into the less conscious. Trust your rhythms and pace, the weave and texture of your process, the spinning of your tales. So long as you continue to write, you are creating your art.

{*See also* Revising, p. 107; Use Practice as Building Blocks, p. 126; Writing Cycles: To Every Thing There Is a Season, p. 116}

THE WRITING LIFE

WRITERS ON DREAMING

WILLIAM STYRON said the whole concept of *Sophie's Choice* was the result, if not of a dream, of a kind of waking vision.

If **AMY TAN** was stuck on the ending of a story, she took the story with her to bed and let it become part of a dream.

ROBERT STONE said, "The process of creating is related to the process of dreaming although when you are writing you're doing it and when you're dreaming it's doing you."

SUE GRAFTON believes that frightening dreams are wonderful. She said they re-create all the physiology she needs in describing her private-eye heroine, Kinsey Millhone, in a dangerous situation.

JORGE LUIS BORGES said that it is written in the kabbalah that when the words in a dream are loud and distinct and seem to come from no particular source, these words are from God.

ALLAN GURGANUS reported that his characters have made guest appearances in his dreams.

Both **JOHN BARTH** and **JAMES W. HALL** told of dreaming words when they're hot and heavy in the writing process. Hall said when these dreams start to come, he tries to wake himself up because they're so boring.

In her collection *Darkness*, **BHARATI MUKHERJEE**'s story "Angela" re-created the image from a dream she had of cutting wings off birds and sewing them together so she could fly.

> The writer by the nature of his profession is a dreamer and a conscious dreamer.
>
> ⮞ CARSON McCULLERS ⮜

ANNE RICE said, "Sometimes dreams show me that my writing should go deeper. Dreams have not so much changed my work as deepened it."

ANNE RIVERS SIDDONS believes that every creative impulse that a working writer has arises out of that dark old country where dreams come from. "You can trust your subconscious to supply you with truly horrendous, wonderful dreams if you're in the middle of something that's disturbing you badly," she said.

MAURICE SENDAK said, "Dreams raise the emotional level of what I'm doing at the moment."

STEPHEN KING reported he uses dreams the way you'd use a mirror to look at something you couldn't see head-on — for example, to look at your hair in the back.

{*See also* Gifts of the Night: How to Use Your Dreams, p. 214}

TRUTH VERSUS FACT

Sometimes you have to lie to tell the truth, and often you can tell a deeper truth by altering the "how it really happened" facts. As a writer, you turn life into fiction in order to write the stories you have to tell; otherwise you may be unable to tell the truth — not necessarily because the truth might be libelous, but more often because of emotional fears: To tell the truth might hurt someone. To tell the truth is to reveal secrets. What will people think if you tell the truth?

> A writer paradoxically seeks the truth and tells lies every step of the way.
>
> ⌒ ANNE LAMOTT ⌒

You fictionalize real-life events because real life is too hot; you're too close. Fiction gives you some distance. Paradoxically, fiction can tell what Tom Spanbauer calls "a truer truth."

In her book *Bird by Bird*, Anne Lamott writes of teaching a writing student whose mother used to punish him by burning him on the stove. "Use it," she tells him. "She's old, though," he says. "Her life has not been a happy one." Lamott advises him to change the mother, change the family, change where they lived. Change everything except the truth of the experience: that when the little boy was naughty, the mother held his hand to the flames.

Make composite characters, alter time frames, change locations, leave out events. Remake your story so you can home in on the truth of what you have to say.

The very process of memory alters the thing being remembered. Facts are colored in the retelling, and even the hue changes with the tellers. Think of how you alter the telling of an event depending on the audience. How you shade and shadow, texture and highlight the same story as you relate it to your mother, your best friend, your therapist, your lawyer, a stranger on a plane. Consider how their version of the same story differs from yours.

Family stories often have different versions:

"After Grandma Leydon's funeral, Grandpa stopped speaking entirely."

"No, no. Grandpa Leydon stopped speaking long before that. He didn't speak to Grandma Leydon for the entire last year she was alive."

"No, that's not how it was. Grandpa Leydon got cancer and had his larynx removed years after Grandma died. He was fine until then. Talked a blue streak."

So the truth of facts may not be the truth of the story. And the facts may have to be changed in order to be truthful.

This points to the difference between the fiction writer and the memoirist. Mary Karr wrote, "The nitty-gritty is that the novelist creates events for truthful interpretation, whereas the memoirist tries to honestly interpret events plagiarized from reality."

Remember, your only obligation as a writer is to tell the truth. "A writer's problem does not change," Ernest Hemingway told us. "He himself changes, but his problem remains the same. It is always how to write truly, and having found what is true, to project it in such a way that it becomes a part of the experience of the person who reads it."

> Illusions, fantasies, deceptions, fevers — these things are possible in a writer, even desired, all in the service of what is true.
>
> ⌁ SUSANNA MOORE ⌁

{*See also* Transferring Real Life to Fiction, p. 201; Truth Is in the Details, p. 54; Writing Memory, p. 96}

WRITING CYCLES:
TO EVERY THING THERE IS A SEASON

Every writer experiences cycles — a productive time, a fallow time. Just like the Bible says, a time to reap and a time to sow. You will be capable of tremendous output and you will be exhausted. Your cycles may run with the course of the moon or be in rhythm with some internal, cellular clock that keeps its own time.

You may notice that sometimes, no matter what, the writing is difficult. Even though you're not stressed, you're present with your writing, you've set aside the time, and you're looking forward to the session, when you put pen to page nothing happens. Or what does happen is boring. Or junk. The words are clumsy and get in each other's way like the sneakered feet of a thirteen-year-old. You experience a dozen false starts and generally just can't get the thing going. Before you scream "writer's block" and phone your therapist for an appointment, consider that this may just be the fallow side of your cycle.

> In my view a writer is a writer not because she writes well and easily, because she has amazing talent, because everything she does is golden. In my view a writer is a writer because even when there is no hope, even when nothing you do shows any sign of promise, you keep writing anyway.
>
> ⟨ JUNOT DÍAZ ⟩

Other times, your day is short by three hours, you've got umpteen dozen things going on, and when you do sit down at the page, you're jittery and not really present. Yet this time, when you begin writing, it flows. Words light upon each other in graceful abandon, your imagery is as rich as crème brûlée with that same crusty, crispy edge. You hardly notice the passage of time; you write nonstop for two hours.

Through writing practice, you'll learn your cycles — when to take advantage of the productive time and when to refill your stores. If you want to actually track your cycles, go back through several months of notebooks and chart the ebb and flow of your writing.

There are a handful of markings that leave an easy trail: Generous, loose handwriting that spreads across the page and large, open lettering, maybe even writing outside the lines vs. small, cramped lettering with many cross-outs, abandoned words, and deserted sentences. Fresh language and vivid images vs. trite words and weary clichés. Page after page of writing in a session vs. a paltry few paragraphs in the same amount of writing time. As you reread the pieces, you'll see right away when you were on and when you were off.

Of course, no chart will give you complete information about your writing history. There's more to writing cycles than the pull of the moon or the beat of an internal rhythm; even the ocean is influenced by storms. However, if you are unable to write, consider that this may be a time of dormancy, like that of an orchard in winter: somewhere, underground in the roots and deep within the heartwood of every apple tree, the idea of apples rests, awaiting the time to begin once

> When I write, I feel like an armless legless man with a crayon in his mouth.
>
> ~ KURT VONNEGUT ~

again the cycle of fruition. Do not judge yourself during this fallow time; accept that it is a time of rest and infuse yourself. Take in, fill up, rejuvenate.

And when you are producing, "give it, give it all, give it now," as Annie Dillard said. Every time.

{*See also* Writer's Block, p. 192; What *Stuck* Looks Like, p. 142; How to Get Unstuck, p. 148}

JUNE 26	Write about being unable to sleep
JUNE 27	"What will die with me when I die…" (after Jorge Luis Borges)
JUNE 28	This is the hand you were dealt
JUNE 29	"I am writing you from a far-off country" (after Henri Michaux)
JUNE 30	Driving through the fog

BEYOND PRACTICE

ON THE ROAD

Complete books have been written "on the road" — John Steinbeck's *Travels with Charley*, William Least Heat-Moon's *Blue Highways*, and Jack Kerouac's *On the Road*, to name just three. This Beyond Practice session urges you to pack your bags and your notebooks and take to the streets or highways or airways. Grab a boat, catch a plane, hop a train. And write.

What may happen is that you'll write about the place you've just left. Henrik Ibsen wrote about Norway while in Italy, James Joyce wrote of Dublin from Paris, where Ernest Hemingway wrote of Detroit. Willa Cather composed her prairie novels in New York City.

Or maybe you'll be like Steinbeck, Heat-Moon, and Kerouac, writing about the road you're traveling from your view just above it, notebook open on the seat beside you. Writing yourself to sleep at night and awaking in the morning with your hand already moving, words and impressions abiding in your mind as if they had been captured in the lair of a dream catcher.

> The more you fling yourself out there, and chase those dreams and miracles, the higher your likelihood of catching one.
>
> ⌐ STEPHANIE ELIZONDO GRIEST ⌐

Travel sets the pen free. Especially when you go it alone. Traveling solo means talking to strangers. Meeting people, asking questions. Of course you're curious; you're a writer. You take in everything, and it's all different — the tilt of the earth, the curve of the horizon, the very color of the sunset. To whom can you say, "Look at that view," when you are alone? You must describe to your notebook the catch of lilac as the sky snags the edge of granite cliff, the turn of hawk balanced on a thermal, its wing afire from the setting sun. When you leave your pals behind, you cannot discuss the details of your job over a meal at the Taverna Totrista. You must taste the *tzatziki*, the resiny flavor of the retsina; you must pay attention to the sensuous whine of the bouzouki and say aloud *Opa!* and smile at the old man dancing. Later, you'll remember the very resonance of your *Opa!* against your rib cage, the scimitar curve of the old man's moustache. This you record in your notebook.

A Navajo chant goes, "Remember what you have seen, because everything forgotten returns to the circling winds." Keep a travel journal; write in it what you observe, what you notice, the names of places and people, cultural impressions and emotional moments. Write of romance, of fear, of connections, and of loneliness. Write what you ate and what you wished you hadn't eaten. Where you felt a complete stranger and where you felt more like yourself than you ever did at home. Write concrete details and sensory perceptions. Scraps of dialogue and descriptions of people. Gather all of it: mementos and menus, maps and moments captured in language, and press them between the pages.

To travel is to see for yourself, to encounter a world outside the accustomed and experience yourself in it. Travel loosens the dust of familiarity and shakes free the folds of the everyday.

You need not take a lengthy trip to experience the effects of travel on your writing. Nor need you go far. A weekend jaunt to the next county or a three-month tour of New Zealand. "I travel not to go anywhere, but to go," said writer-adventurer Robert Louis Stevenson. "I travel for travel's sake. The great affair is to move."

A few prompts for the road:

- I can't explain . . .
- Write about first light
- Write about the random possibility of miracles
- "I am in a state of surrender" (after Donald Rawley)
- Midsummer night
- This is the sound of loneliness

{ JULY }

Literature is an act of conscience.
It's up to us to rebuild with memories,
with ruins, and with moments of grace.

— ELIE WIESEL

GUIDELINE 7

KISS YOUR FROGS

It happens to every writer: sloppy, rambling, unintelligible, boring writing that is going anywhere but where you want. If you write at all, know that you're going to produce some stuff that's way to the left of good, lopsided and croaking on some withering lily pad. It's the frog-kissing phenomenon of creative writing, and it happens to the best of us, even to seasoned pros.

First-draft writing doesn't have to be good, it won't always be good, and even when it is good, among the good will be some not-so-good. For many writers, understanding and accepting this fact has a powerfully freeing effect. Natalie Goldberg has given what some writing practitioners say is the most valuable advice they've ever received: "You're free to write the worst junk in America," she says. Anne Lamott also has a name for that rough stuff we all write. She calls it "shitty first drafts." It's the swampy, mucky stuff that holds little promise for happily-ever-after.

At any given writing session you may write something you like, or your writing may embarrass you in its awful triteness. Sometimes you won't be able to put a coherent sentence together, and other times your writing will be fresh, creative, even elegant. The point is, just show up at the page, no matter what.

Remember, this is just practice. You write what you write. Besides, who can say from the marshy edge of any pond which frog gets transformed and which kiss holds magic?

TIP OF THE MONTH

In writing…the less conformity the better — except, perhaps, when it comes to spelling and punctuation.

— SCOTT SPENCER

BEING VULNERABLE ON THE PAGE

Writers expose more of themselves than any other artists. When we write about what matters to us, we unveil our deepest feelings. Sometimes even to ourselves and often when we least expect it. When we write about human frailties, we are writing about the fragile scraps of ourselves. Our words tell the truth about more than what we're writing; they also tell the truth about us.

No wonder writing often feels dangerous, makes you lurch from your chair, pace the room, and phone your best friend just to hear a reassuring voice. "Hi. What are you doing?" [Pause] "Me? Oh, nothing. Just writing." Meantime, the truth of your exposed and bleeding self spreads line by incriminating line across thirteen inches of cold white monitor. And that cursor just keeps blinking, reminding you you're not finished yet. Your notebook lies open on your desk, yammering your secrets to any passerby. You pour a cup of coffee, smoke a cigarette, and snack on anything that might alter the way you feel.

Being vulnerable on the page is one of the risks of the job — it comes with the territory, as with performing a high-wire act with a new partner and without a net in a drafty circus tent. And in all likelihood, it's not something that will go away. You

> I had to get over my fear of running through the world naked and learn to say, "Take me or leave me."
>
> ⌒ STEVEN SPIELBERG ⌒

may become accustomed to the feeling, but you'll never escape the vulnerability. John Cheever said, "I think that endeavoring to be a serious writer is quite a dangerous career."

What to do? Take a drink of water, breathe deeply, stretch, go ahead and call a friend, then get back to the writing. A little distance may make you feel safer, but the very fact that you are feeling vulnerable means you're writing close to the bone. Stay with it.

{*See also* Take Risks, p. 132; Tell Your Secrets, p. 212; Breathe, p. 215}

HOW TO TELL WHEN THE WRITER-SELF IS PRESENT

The writer-self is the part of you that is unequivocally for your writing and believes in you absolutely. This is the sweet voice that urges you to put pen to paper and tells you writing is noble and necessary and names the many ways it adds to the quality of life. More than that, it says the work of the writer is "essential for human evolution," as Norman Cousins put it. Write, it says to you.

> Make a habit of putting your observations into words and gradually this will become instinct.
>
> ⮑ GEOFF DYER ⮐

You can tell that your writer-self is present when:

- You look forward to your writing time and go on the arm of joy to the special writing place you created.
- You're not writing — it's before or after your writing time — but anticipatory or lingering thoughts of writing come to you, prologues or epilogues to doing the work.
- You read other writers and, while you're reading for pleasure or inspiration or to learn, you also notice their execution of the craft.
- You can't help yourself — if a scribble of paper is there along with a pen, you write something. Words or phrases, an image, or the line of a poem. Crayons and paper at a restaurant table make you giddy.
- You're writing, time passes — an hour, two, three — and you're hardly aware.
- You make plans for a holiday or retreat, a weekend getaway. It includes writing.
- You'd rather be with your writing friends — writing together, talking about writing — than with anyone else doing anything else.
- You remember people at a writing workshop not by name but by something they wrote.

- You think the most important Oscar is the award for screenwriting. Same with the Tonys (playwriting). Even the Nobel Prize in Literature ranks above the others, as far as you're concerned.
- You hang out at readings, book signings, and author appearances not just to hear the writer read but to be in the presence of another writer, to connect with your own kind.
- Before you drift off to sleep or just when you awaken, your first thought or last thought is about your writing.
- Your bookshelves sag with books by writers about writing, interviews with writers, how-tos on writing, and biographies and memoirs of writers.
- The many, many periodicals you subscribe to include magazines that feature quality writing, obscure literary journals and small press quarterlies, and trade publications about writers and writing.
- Your Internet bookmarks run into the dozens — most of them writing sites. You read blogs of writers you admire.
- You write every day (or as near to that as you can get).
- Your stamina is amazing. You get up to write at 5:30 every morning, or there you are at o'dark hundred, writing beneath the sagging moon. And you still have energy to work your day job.

Your writer-self may not always have priority in your life — there are, after all, falling in love, being with family, honoring the Sacred — but when he or she is present, pay attention. This voice comes from a true part of you.

JULY	6	Write about broken bones
JULY	7	"I remember once in _____"
JULY	8	A dark December day
JULY	9	"Only here. Only now." (after Lucille Clifton)
JULY	10	They told me it would be like this

USE PRACTICE AS BUILDING BLOCKS

Most all the daily writing practice prompts allow you to continue to develop the raw material of a project you are working on. In fact, using the prompt for that day, you may enter into the piece in a way that would not have been possible had you first thought about what you wanted to write. Writing on the topic is like choosing "door number three." You don't know what's behind the curtain until it's lifted.

Keeping your focus within the confines of your project, let the writing topic be your starting place. If you're writing fiction, write the prompt from the point of view of one of your characters. Change the pronoun from *I* or *you* to *he* or *she*, or use the character's name. For example, if the prompt is "Write about your neighborhood at five o'clock," write about your character's neighborhood in late afternoon. Let the dialogue prompt "You'll be sorry" be the character's dialogue or something another character says to them. A prompt can even be a question you, as author, pose to your character (such as, "Where were you last night?").

If you're writing nonfiction — memoir or personal narrative — and the prompt doesn't appear to fit (for example, "I walked into the Maverick Bar in Farmington, New Mexico"), write about a time you walked into any bar, or a time you wanted to walk into a bar, or a time you didn't walk into a bar. Write about a time you were in New Mexico or wanted to be. Turn the whole thing around and begin with "I never walked into the Maverick Bar in Farmington, New Mexico, but I..." and continue in whatever direction you want to go. Use the prompt as starting blocks from which you push off to begin your laps around the writing practice track. In rewriting you'll decide whether to lop off references to a bar, the Maverick or any other, or any talk of New Mexico.

> When I start I am in total limbo. I don't have any idea where the story is going or what is going to happen or why I am writing it.
>
> — ISABEL ALLENDE —

Several members of my Brown Bag and Thursday Writers groups have used practice prompts to write portions of their novels or stories or memoirs. In fact, many scenes in my own novels had their genesis in these groups.

{*See also* Rereading Your Practice Pages, p. 185; When Characters Appear, p. 187; Revising, p. 107}

MENTORS AND HEROES

CHATEAUBRIAND was **VICTOR HUGO**'s inspiration and **MARCEL PROUST**'s hero.

The catalyst for **EDNA O'BRIEN** was a lecture she heard in London on **F. SCOTT FITZGERALD** and **ERNEST HEMINGWAY**.

MAY SARTON was inspired by novelist **VIRGINIA WOOLF**.

UMBERTO ECO's *The Name of the Rose* inspired **A. S. BYATT**, who said, "One could be at once both very serious and quite funny, and write a detective story in the bargain."

From **ANNIE DILLARD**'s book *The Writing Life*: "**HEMINGWAY** studied, as models, the novels of **KNUT HAMSUN** and **IVAN TURGENEV**. **ISAAC BASHEVIS SINGER**, as it happened, also chose **HAMSUN** and **TURGENEV** as models. **RALPH ELLISON** studied **HEMINGWAY** and **GERTRUDE STEIN**. **THOREAU** loved **HOMER**; **EUDORA WELTY** loved **CHEKHOV**. **FAULKNER** described his debt to **SHERWOOD ANDERSON** and **JOYCE**; **E. M. FORSTER**, his debt to **JANE AUSTEN** and **PROUST**."

APOLLINAIRE influenced **ANDRÉ BRETON**, who influenced **ALLEN GINSBERG** and **WILLIAM CARLOS WILLIAMS**, who was, at the time, a local underground celebrity who encouraged **GINSBERG**'s early writing.

TRUMAN CAPOTE was influential in **JOSEPH WAMBAUGH**'s writing of *The Onion Field*. "My God," he told Wambaugh, "that's a marvelous story. I wish I could write that."

JOHN CHEEVER was the inspiration for **ETHAN CANIN**, who says, "Cheever's rhythmic elongation of epiphany in the midst of quiet suburban life brought me over and over again to a sense of longing. At first it was a longing to read. Later it became a longing to write."

RAY BRADBURY made up a genealogy, a sort of family tree: "I often think of **ROBERT FROST** as my wonderful grandfather and **WILLA CATHER** as my grandmother. **EUDORA WELTY** is an eccentric cousin of mine, and

EDGAR RICE BURROUGHS might even be my father. JULES VERNE I remember as a marvelous uncle who used to bring me fabulous toys that ran underwater and through the skies and off to the far planets. Somewhere along the line JOHN STEINBECK is my older brother and ERNEST HEMINGWAY a still older brother than that. WILLIAM FAULKNER is a very wise old second uncle. A teacher would be ALDOUS HUXLEY."

> No one ever told me to become a writer; I blame myself.
>
> ⮜ TOM GRIMES ⮞

Who are your mentors and heroes? Whose work do you love? Which writers do you admire? In her book *Making a Literary Life*, Carolyn See urges us to write a "charming note" every day, five days a week, for the rest of our lives, to a writer, an editor, or even an agent whose professional work or reputation we admire. She tells us these notes are "like paper airplanes sailing around the world saluting the writer" and saying, "Your work is good and admirable." She says the notes are also saying, "I exist, too."

Try creating your own family tree of mentors and heroes who have influenced you.

JULY 11	In her fantasies about _____
JULY 12	Write about staying awake all night
JULY 13	Lost in the shadows of time past
JULY 14	A black-and-white photograph
JULY 15	Write about a flying dream

HONOR YOURSELF AS WRITER

Putting in time at writing practice is only one of the ways to honor yourself as writer. This list offers several more.

> Remember you love writing. It wouldn't be worth it if you didn't. If the love fades, do what you need to and get it back.
>
> ⌒ A. L. KENNEDY ⌒

- Name yourself *writer*. When people ask what you do, say, "I am a writer." Writing may not be the way you support yourself, but identifying yourself by your day job doesn't give your writing the position it deserves. One person may say, "I'm a writer who supports herself as a paralegal." Another, "I'm a writer. And I earn a living as a massage therapist." When you name yourself *writer* first, you affirm the place writing holds in your life.

- Make a place for your writing, and furnish it with materials that support you and your writing. A good desk or table, a comfortable chair, ample light that is flattering to your writing, shelves or bookcases. Keep the space sacred and go there joyfully.

- Get the equipment and accoutrements you need — a home computer or laptop, a printer you can depend on, an extra ink cartridge or two. Notebooks, journals, pens, paper you like. A good dictionary, thesaurus, and other reference materials. This is not to imply you must have the latest equipment to really be a writer. Not only can high tech be expensive, it doesn't guarantee your writing will be any better. Remember, Shakespeare had only a quill pen and candlelight.

- Make time for studying and practicing your craft: attend writing groups, workshops, writers' conferences, classes, and lectures. Go on writing retreats.

- Schedule time with other writers: get together before or after your group or make time just for hanging out, meet for coffee or a beer, walk a trail together. This is a time for discussing your own writing and writing in general, meandering conversations or meaningful dialogue. Either way, this is quality time.

- Read your writing to others; give a poem to someone whom you know would appreciate it; read your pieces to family and friends and read your work at open readings.

- Transfer writing from your notebook to your computer and print it out. A piece appears more professional when it's printed; it says, "This is a serious piece of writing." File the printed pieces in an orderly way, harboring them in three-ring binders, labeled and berthed on a shelf. Back up your writing on an external drive.

- Submit material for publication. As intimidating as the whole process can be — doing the market research, writing the cover letter, preparing the pristine manuscript, and then sealing the envelope and immediately knowing you left out page three; releasing the package into the black hole of a mail slot; or hitting SEND on an email with an attached submission whose formatting you worry will be lost somewhere in the cyberspace of the transfer — in spite of all this, you submit your writing for publication because you believe it is good and you believe writing needs an audience to be complete. Submitting your material for publication honors the writing and honors you as writer.

- Celebrate when you've completed a work or hit a significant marker: a chapter finished, first draft completed, difficult scene written. Some writers celebrate with champagne; others, blended mochas; and still others, a trip to the bookstore. Choose your treat. You deserve it.

- Accept compliments gracefully. When someone tells you they like your writing or that your words touched them, no need to demur, explain what's wrong, or go into a lengthy discourse about what you really meant to write. Simply say thank you.

JULY 16	"The catalogue of my betrayals" (after Tony Hoagland)
JULY 17	She took the red-eye
JULY 18	Write about the night wind
JULY 19	This is the geography of her (his) body
JULY 20	Oranges and apples

IF YOU WANT TO WRITE

BY BRENDA UELAND

1. Know that you have talent, are original and have something important to say.

2. Know that it is good to work. Work with love and think of liking it when you do it. It is easy and interesting. It is a privilege. There is nothing hard about it but your anxious vanity and fear of failure.

3. Write freely, recklessly, in first drafts.

4. Tackle anything you want to — novels, plays, anything. Only remember Blake's admonition: "Better to strangle an infant in its cradle than nurse unacted desires."

5. Don't be afraid of writing bad stories. To discover what is wrong with a story write two new ones and then go back to it.

6. Don't fret or be ashamed of what you have written in the past. How I always suffered from this! How I would regurgitate out of my memory (and still do) some nauseous little lumps of things I had written! But don't do this. Go on to the next. And fight against this tendency, which is much of it due not to splendid modesty, but a lack of self-respect. We are too ready (women especially) not to stand by what we have said or done. Often it is a way of forestalling criticism, saying hurriedly: "I know it is awful!" before anyone else does. Very bad and cowardly. It is so conceited and timid to be ashamed of one's mistakes. Of *course* they are mistakes. Go on to the next.

7. Try to discover your true, honest, untheoretical self.

8. Don't think of yourself as an intestinal tract and tangle of nerves in the skull, that will not work unless you drink coffee. Think of yourself as incandescent power, illuminated perhaps and forever talked to by God and his messengers. Remember how wonderful you are, what a miracle! Think if Tiffany's made a mosquito, how wonderful we would think it was!

9. If you are never satisfied with what you write, that is a good sign. It means your vision can see so far that it is hard to come up to it. Again I say, the only unfortunate people are the glib ones, immediately satisfied with their work. To them, the ocean is only knee-deep.

10. When discouraged, remember what Van Gogh said: "If you hear a voice within you saying: You are no painter, then paint by all means, lad, and that voice will be silenced, but only by working."

11. Don't be afraid of yourself when you write. Don't check-rein yourself. If you are afraid of being sentimental, say, for heaven's sake be as sentimental as you can or feel like being! Then you will probably pass through to the other side and slough off sentimentality because you understand it at last and really don't care about it.

12. Don't always be appraising yourself, wondering if you are better or worse than other writers. "I will not Reason & Compare," said Blake; "my business is to Create." Besides, since you are like no other being ever created since the beginning of Time, you are incomparable.

TAKE RISKS

Writing means taking risks. If you're not willing to take the risks, chances are your writing will be bland and boring — even to yourself. However, to take such risks requires "the ongoing courage for self-discovery," said Harlan Ellison. "The act of writing with serious intent involves enormous personal risk. It means one will walk forever on the tightrope, with each new step presenting the possibility of learning a truth about oneself that is too terrible to bear."

Of course, we never discover a truth that is too terrible to bear. We only fear that we will. Or that we will expose something of ourselves to others that will be too terrible for them to bear, and we will be judged, perhaps rejected.

> If you want to write, to really create anything, you have to risk falling on your face.
>
> — ALLEGRA GOODMAN —

Contradictory as it may sound, writing with others is one good way to begin taking risks. There is something about a group setting that engenders bravery — safety in numbers, maybe. Also, listening to the risks others take in their writing can mark a trail to your own cliff edges.

Janet Fitch told members of her advanced fiction workshop to "stay in the room," meaning don't let your characters or yourself leave the scene before it's complete. In real life when there's danger or conflict the safest action may be to hightail it, but in writing, safety is not a desired ingredient. So even if you have to take a few deep breaths and write paragraphs around what you need to say, "stay in the room" until you've written it.

Take courage, be brave. In taking the risks we find our true and honest voice. This is the way to freedom.

{*See also* Avoiding the Truth, p. 98; How to Tell When the Censor Is Present, p. 175; Being Vulnerable on the Page, p. 123}

JULY 21	Trying to explain	
JULY 22	"At the end we prayed for death" (after Mary Karr)	
JULY 23	She said to call her anytime	
JULY 24	Write about the expectation of pleasure	
JULY 25	We said we'd never speak of it	

GIFTS FROM THE MUSE: PHRASES, IMAGES, AND OTHER KINDNESSES

You're working in your garden, and a buoyant phrase alights upon your shoulder; in the shower, the perfect solution to the story you're writing suddenly comes to you; while you're driving down the freeway, a poem appears, nearly intact. This is Muse mojo, and who knows how it happens.

Perhaps because you've primed the pump with the work you've already done, relaxing in the shower loosens ideas that were caught between the folds of your brain or in the cramp of your muscles. Maybe the rhythmic step of your foot upon a dusty footpath sets down a beat that cannot be resisted, or the comforting ease of lowering dishes into hot soapy water calls forth memories of other kitchens, other times. It seems when you turn to mindless things, you create an incubator for the intuition. "When I was painting the downstairs hall I thought of a novel to write," said Anne Tyler.

These images, phrases, and other kindnesses are gifts from the Muse. Her timing is not always impeccable, but her gifts are always delicious, albeit perishable. Grab them while you can. Don't rely on your memory; keep pen and paper nearby.

Writers I know have as many sets of note-taking necessities around the house as it's rumored Frank Sinatra had reading glasses. Notepads and pens in the bedroom on the nightstand (a poet I know jotted iambics on his pillowcase that transferred in the night to his cheek); a waterproof pen and non-absorbent paper on a shelf just outside the shower curtain; a magic slate dangling magnetically from the refrigerator door; three-by-five cards and felt-tips sealed inside baggies and kept with the gardening tools; goofy-looking notepads affixed to the dashboard of the car; tiny spiral-bound notepads no bigger than your palm stashed in a hip pocket along with a golf-scoring pencil; sticky notes affixed to the most unlikely of surfaces — decorator pillows, dry cleaning bags, dinner plates, makeup mirrors — and, when all else fails, patches of skin exposed beneath shirt cuffs and gym socks.

> Writing is a gift we carry back to our ancestors, like fire.
>
> ⌒ JUSTIN CRONIN ⌒

{*See also* Saying Yes to the Muse, p. 110}

BETTER VERBS, FEWER ADVERBS

"Use better verbs!" came the critique on one of my manuscripts. I reread it, embarrassed to realize how often I had used the verb *was*. Once I noticed it, the word stuck out like the proverbial sore thumb. *Was* was everywhere, like dandelions infecting a lawn.

How easy to use *was*. How that word just slides off our fingertips and onto the page as we merrily write along. Maybe the word actually resides in our fingers and shows up as automatic writing. Maybe it asserts itself like our heart, an involuntary muscle. Though in *was*'s case, there's not much muscle involved. *Was* is a weakling of a verb. So is its present tense form, *is*. Both versions are forms of the verb *to be*.

The *to be* verb comes in various forms (*there are, it is, we were, I was*), including present and past tense and a couple of participles, all of which we won't get into here. They fall in the category of passive verbs that many of us slip into when we get a little lazy or sloppy or in a hurry to finish. Though there are times when some form of *to be* can be a good choice, make sure you use them by choice and not through neglect. *Woe Is I*, by Patricia T. O'Conner, and other books on English usage untangle this and other grammatical complications. Let's just say active verbs are almost always preferable to weak ones. Active verbs are more direct and more colorful, which brings us back to the scolding I got on my poor manuscript.

Verbs are the combustible material of the language; they create the action, they invigorate the writing. Verbs contain the energy of sentences; they move the sentences forward. Think of common verbs like *cry, walk,* or *plan*. Look at the stronger images you create when you use verbs that paint a more defined picture for the reader: *weep, limp,* or *scheme*. Here's a lovely line from F. Scott Fitzgerald's *The Great Gatsby*: "Inside, the crimson room bloomed with light." Or this, from Barbara Kingsolver's "High Tide in Tucson": "Bees hummed at the edge of the water hole, nosing up to the water, their abdomens pulsing like tiny hydraulic pumps." Those are the kind of verbs my writing teacher had in mind when she scrawled her directive on my pages.

> Every word is there for a reason, and if not, I cross it out. I cut adjectives, adverbs, and every word which is there just to make an effect.
>
> ⮜ JERZY KOSINSKI ⮞

Now about adverbs: Mostly, they're not needed. Often the -*ly* word following the verb is redundant — televisions that blare loudly or jaws that clench tightly. Or maybe you're attempting to shore up a weak verb by tacking on an adverb, as in, "Alice ate her lunch quickly." Quickly, what verbs can you come up with that show how Alice ate her lunch? So when you call in the *was* police to check your sentences, give them extra duty of trailing those adverbs. Use the Find and Replace tool on your word processing program to help you locate the minor offenders by searching for *ly* or for *was*, *is*, and the like, and replace them with livelier or stronger words.

But what to use as substitutes for all those *was*es? How to bulk up those weak verbs? This is where the crafting of the writing begins. Go ahead and write your practice piece, verbing as you will. Then as you reread, underline all the verbs; notice the words that show some spunk, lift heavy loads, block and tackle, tap-dance, and generally liven up your sentences; these are the keepers, the show, don't tell–ers. Next, notice all those boring, clichéd verbs, the adverbs, the *was*es and other forms of *to be*, the *had had*s and *would be*s. These are the ones you want to change. And you do it verb by verb.

Here are some suggestions and exercises to enliven your verbology. (I just made that word up.)

- Use your thesaurus and dictionary.
- Use your imagination.
- Try this exercise: list all the verbs that go with a certain activity — cooking, for example, or gardening. Sewing. Swimming. Writing.
- List all the jobs you've had and verbalize your activities.
- List all the actions you've taken so far today.
- Read really good writers and pay attention to their verb-crafting.
- Instead of trying to think of better words, close your eyes and picture the image, then come up with words that describe the action.
- Write a sentence, then change the verb to create different pictures. For example, "Benny walked across the room." What verbs can

you use that show more clearly how Benny crossed the room? Note: this is what we mean when we say, "Show, don't tell."

P.S. Don't be so clever with your verbs that you draw attention to them. Like a really good dinner party, they should be beautiful and delicious without any hint of the work it took to make it happen.

{*See also* Auditioning Words, p. 32; Wordplay, p. 202; About Language, p. 48; When the Words Aren't Working: A Helping Hand, p. 169; Show, Don't Tell, p. 78}

JULY 26	Taking an unfamiliar road
JULY 27	Something moves in the distance
JULY 28	"I was meant to be someone else" (after Philip Levine)
JULY 29	Write about changing clothes
JULY 30	When we returned . . .
JULY 31	"A random selection of bad habits" (after Louis Jenkins)

BEYOND PRACTICE

"A JUG OF WINE, A LOAF OF BREAD — A NOTEBOOK"

A writer doesn't need much. For Persian poet Omar Khayyám it was "A book of verses underneath the bough," the wine, the bread, and "thou beside me singing in the wilderness," which were for him, enough. With these few effects, wilderness became paradise.

For those who accept the invitation, this Beyond Practice takes writers to a simpler place to find the richness within the moment, to transform the plain into the sublime.

For the morning or afternoon, pack away into your backpack or satchel simple supplies: bread and cheese, some uncomplicated fruit — grapes or cherries, an apple. Bring spring water or wine. Choose a book of verse — Walt Whitman's *Leaves of Grass*, Elizabeth Barrett Browning's *Sonnets from the Portuguese*, Khayyám's *Rubaiyat*, if you please. Or one of your own well-thumbed favorites. Gather your notebook and pens. Let your "thou" be a soul-connected writing friend.

Take all this and go into the wilderness, a place far enough from the city so the traffic noise cannot reach you, so you don't look upon freeways or streets with stoplights, or any streets at all. No parks with playgrounds where children screech and yammer. No basketball courts or soccer fields. Go beyond all that to a quiet place where, if you hear anything, it will be a chorale of birds, the tumble of stream, the sweet whisper of wind in leaves.

> We write to taste life twice, in the moment and in retrospection.
>
> ⌒ ANAÏS NIN ⌒

Find a gracious tree that welcomes you beneath its green and spread your simple feast before you. Don't just eat; savor. With all your senses. Read aloud from your book of verses; close your eyes and know this is paradise. Don't be in a rush to begin your writing. Let the verses you have read sink into your bones, close your eyes, and breathe the words. Read again, aloud to your partner; let "thou" read to you. Then, when you are ready, open your notebook and begin writing. Allow a generous, unhurried time, and when you are finished, read aloud to each other again, this time reading what you have written, giving your own writing the same loving attention you gave the master's.

Since you brought the bread and wine, we'll provide the prompts.

- These are the things I lost
- Write about the shadows of afternoon
- This is what she asked for
- It was the night of the crocus moon
- Write about sleeping outside

{AUGUST}

At its best, the sensation of writing is that of unmerited grace.
— ANNIE DILLARD

GUIDELINE 8

TELL THE TRUTH

Every time you write you have an opportunity to tell the truth. Sometimes it's only through writing that you can know the truth, which may be one of the reasons we write in the first place. "The only time I know that something is true is at the moment I discover it in the act of writing," said French novelist Jean Malaquais.

Writing a truth sets up a physical commotion: there's a humming deep in the throat, little hairs on the back of the neck rise and tremble, goose pimples (my grandmother called them "truth bumps") freckle the arms. Breathing changes. This is why it's good to be tuned in to your body while you write. "This is important," it's saying. "Pay attention."

The truth can also be risky. Andre Dubus said, "When I'm writing — that's when I face the exposure, that's when the right word comes, or the temptation to use the wrong word and duck out, the temptation to skip something. That's when I always have to bear down and try to write as closely to what is the truth as I can feel with my senses and with my heart."

Be willing to go to the scary places that cause your hand to tremble and your handwriting to get a little out of control. Be willing to tell your secrets.

It's risky, but if you don't write about it, you're chancing writing that is glib, shallow, or bland.

Go to the edge of what feels safe and step off. We always use a net in writing practice.

TIP OF THE MONTH

Readers don't want to merely read about your characters and the world you've created. They want to smell it, touch it and taste it.

— JANET FITCH

AUGUST	1	Nothing lasts
AUGUST	2	This is what it cost
AUGUST	3	"…the details of unremarkable days" (after Revan Schendler)
AUGUST	4	Write what is underneath good intentions
AUGUST	5	It was a family story

SPIRITUAL CONNOTATIONS OF WRITING PRACTICE

"Writers all devise ways to approach that place where they expect to make the contact, where they become the conduit, or where they engage in this mysterious process," said Toni Morrison.

Practice is more than running the scales, shooting the hoops, doing the drills; it has a deeper component. Coming again and again to the same place, mindful and with intention, writing practice becomes in itself a spiritual act. When you enter into your writer's soul, you are treading upon sacred ground.

Consider what you do when you practice writing: You set aside a special time when you will focus all your attention on your practice; you give yourself over to this time. Opening your notebook, you open yourself to possibility, to intuition. Inspiration. You breathe in. *Inspiration* — an animating action or influence. You begin writing and lose yourself to the only time there is: Now. You are wholly with yourself, alive and present in the moment, writing, transcribing what comes from within. When you finish writing and look up from your notebook, there is a sense that you have been elsewhere; it may take a moment to return fully to this world. You feel a certain elation, a completeness.

> Being a writer does not have the global reach of being a canonized saint but, at its best, writing is a deeply spiritual act that can have a profound effect upon the practitioner.
>
> ⮐ PHYLLIS THEROUX ⮐

"Creativity is an experience — to my eye, a spiritual experience. It does not matter which way you think of it: creativity leading to spirituality or spirituality leading to creativity. In fact, I do not make a distinction between the two," said Julia Cameron, creator of *The Artist's Way*.

{*See also* Ten Daily Habits That Make a (Good) Writer, p. 39}

WHAT *STUCK* LOOKS LIKE

We've given the term *writer's block* so much power that even talking about it can scare us into one. But *stuck*, that's another matter. *Stuck* is a state of being that many writers experience. Think of rear wheels in mud, rings on swollen fingers. *Stuck* is a manageable, fixable annoyance that simply needs something solid beneath it, a little grease, maybe.

> It's amazing the terrors, the magic, the prayers, the straitening shyness that assails one.
>
> ⌒ JOHN STEINBECK ⌒

Here's a list of some of the disguises *stuck* wears, along with some suggestions for unsticking yourself. (See the accompanying list, How to Get Unstuck, p. 148, for more general ideas.)

- You've written yourself into a corner. Got your characters into a jam, and the only way out is too contrived or far-fetched, straining even your own willingness to suspend disbelief.
  1. Play "What if . . ." and write out all kinds of solutions to the problem. Never mind how contrived or far-fetched they seem; just brainstorm the ideas. Take a few of the more promising ones out for a spin.
  2. Hit the rewind button. Backtrack your story to where the problem started, and take another run at it. (Play "What if . . ." at this point.)
- You're out of ideas for new scenes and don't know where to start the next piece.
  1. This is one of the main purposes of the daily writing prompts. Do a practice session, freewriting from one of the writing prompts. Use your characters' voices if you're writing fiction.
  2. Make a "to do" list for your character, then start writing from one of the items, especially if there's a "to do" listing that involves another character.
  3. In her book *Bird by Bird*, Anne Lamott suggests sending your character out on the streets — to the grocery store, to get a

haircut or a pack of cigarettes. Follow him or her; see what happens.

4. Every character wants something. What is he or she going to do to get it?

5. Go to a memory, a "first time." Write about something lost.

- You keep rehashing the same stuff, simply restating what you've already written.

1. Try a new genre. If you usually write fiction, try nonfiction, or write an essay or a personal narrative piece. If you're a poet, try expanding into fiction or creative nonfiction. Write a play. A screenplay. A monologue or performance piece.

2. If your characters are always the same, try something different. Instead of writing from the point of view of a thirtysomething female, give voice to an old man. Write the opposite of what you usually write: gender, age, geography, physical appearance, politics. Some advise to write what you know; Tom Robbins told workshop participants, "Don't write what you know; write anything you can imagine."

> At the beginning of a novel, a writer needs confidence, but after that what's required is persistence.
>
> ⌒ WALTER KIRN ⌒

- You write around what needs to be written, avoiding the real stuff with distractions and diversions.

1. There's a saying in writing groups when someone is tap-dancing around the truth. "Don't leave the room," participants

AUGUST   6   The view from the top
AUGUST   7   "In my dream I was the first to arrive"
              (after Thomas Smith)
AUGUST   8   Everything means something
AUGUST   9   The way of light on water
AUGUST 10   It's either the beginning or the ending

say, meaning stay in the piece even if it's uncomfortable, even if it makes you sweat and squirm in your chair. Stay in the room and write what needs to be written. John Dufresne suggests "Velcro pants."

2. Write nose-on, blatant stuff and get it all out on paper. Never mind that it's neither graceful nor elegant; just write it. All the hard, stinging, painful, ugly words of it. Write it trite and write it long. Just write it. Now, go back and clean it up, fix it, rewrite it, and polish it. Keep the good, strong, powerful truth; get rid of the sloppy, repetitious, cliché-ridden purple stuff. Give yourself a reward. This is a very courageous act.

> The problem with creative writing is essentially one of concentration.
>
> ⌒ STEPHEN SPENDER ⌒

3. Use a timed writing to get the piece down, putting the prompt or "I want to write about . . ." at the top of your page. Somehow the intensity and focus of writing within a fixed time helps push the words out. If you don't finish in one session, reset the timer and go at it again.

- You can't seem to finish anything. You write a few pages or a few chapters, a stanza or two of a poem, then put the piece away and start something new.

1. Make a commitment to yourself and to someone else to finish the piece, no matter what. Even if you know it won't be perfect and it isn't what you intended to write. Make the commitment, then hang in there. (Better make a deadline for yourself, too.)

2. Promise yourself a reward for finishing. Make it something you value, something you've been wanting for a long time. Absolutely give it to yourself when you complete the project. Make a big production out of it. (We know this is bribery. Do it anyway. You deserve it.)

3. Join a writing group or take a class with the intention of writing through something beginning to end. Ask for the support of the group.

- You do great on synopsis or outline but can't get into the full-out writing of the piece.

    1. Instead of writing the synopsis or outline, just start right in on the writing. Could be you're tired of the thing before you've even written it. There's nothing to learn, no surprises.

    2. When you tell the story the way you think it should be told, you rob the story of the opportunity to tell itself. "I write to find the story," says Wally Lamb. Don't worry that you don't know what the piece is about; just write and let the "about-ness" appear. Be willing to be lost.

- You are intimidated by the idea of writing a long, sustained piece, whether long means a 1,500-word essay, a 5,000-word story, or a 300-page novel.

> I think when I get blocked it's when I have something to say but I don't want to say it.
>
> ⌐ PAUL SIMON ⌐

    1. Write in short bursts, a paragraph at a time, just one scene. Anne Lamott calls these "short assignments." Don't consider the distance between beginning and ending; just write today's assignment.

    2. Set a goal of a page a day, or 400 words a day, or set a time limit: twenty minutes, an hour. Make your goals or time limits manageable. Do it a day at a time.

- You continue to edit and rewrite the same piece or the same section over and over, never adding any new material or starting anything else.

    1. Put the project you've already written (and rewritten) away. Work on only new material without any rewriting, writing only in your notebook. Don't enter any of it into the computer, and don't go back and edit the previous day's writing. Do this for a month. Don't worry about the rawness of it. You can clean it up later. Just keep writing.

    2. Accept — no, *really* accept — there's no such thing as perfect.

- You attend workshop after workshop, taking the same old material out for another go-around of read-and-critique, but you never write anything new or incorporate the critique you received. Or you keep sending much-rejected pieces out to different publications.

1. Try the suggestions listed under the preceding *stuck* description. And remember this old adage: Writers write.

2. Instead of signing up for another workshop, spend the time you would be at the workshop writing new material. If part of what you love about being at a workshop is being in a new place and interacting with other writers, invite a writing friend to go away on a retreat with you (*see* Beyond Practice: Writing Retreats, p. 239).

> A writer is a person for whom writing is more difficult than it is for other people.
>
> ⮞ THOMAS MANN ⮜

3. If you've sent the same piece out more than a dozen times without rewriting any of it and all you've gotten are rejections, consider that (a) you may be sending it out to the wrong markets, or, more likely, (b) you need to take another look at it and do some rewrites.

- You talk about writing all the time, but you don't put pen to paper.

    1. Sign up for a class or workshop where group exercises are part of the process and homework is assigned.

    2. Make writing dates with friends, and do the prompt of the day together (*see* Beyond Practice: A Writing Date, p. 25).

- You make writing dates with yourself, but you don't keep them.

    1. Include a friend on the date. It's easier to show up if you know someone is expecting you.

    2. Change the appointment to a time that works better for you — if not morning, lunchtime. If not lunchtime, right after work. Make your dates very brief — ten or fifteen minutes. Anyone can write for ten or fifteen minutes.

- You often sign up for classes or groups but drop out after a few sessions.

    1. Know what's expected of you before you sign up. If one of the requirements is to bring six or eight or ten pages of work

to every session, make sure you have the time and are willing to commit to the workload.

2.   Commit to being part of the group and showing up each time.
     If you're having difficulties, talk it over with the instructor or
     group leader rather than simply dropping out. Be willing to
     ask yourself the real reasons you stopped attending.

If you follow the path backward from all these stuck places, you'll find
that many of them are rooted in fear. Anxiety is a natural and necessary part
of creativity. "If you are to create," Eric Maisel writes in *Fearless Creating*,
"you must invite anxiety in." What is necessary, he tells us, is to manage the
anxiety.

<table>
<tr><td>**AUGUST 11**</td><td>"Nevertheless it's still summer" (after Charles Wright)</td></tr>
<tr><td>**AUGUST 12**</td><td>Write about taking the long way around</td></tr>
<tr><td>**AUGUST 13**</td><td>Something you saved</td></tr>
<tr><td>**AUGUST 14**</td><td>"Are you alone?" he asked.</td></tr>
<tr><td>**AUGUST 15**</td><td>A shifting of shadows</td></tr>
</table>

HOW TO GET UNSTUCK

Still stuck? Try some of these ideas to get rolling again.

1. Take a walk.
2. Take a shower.
3. Take a long, luxurious bath, with music, candles, and bath salts.
4. Wash the dishes. Or work in the yard. Sweep the porch.
5. Take a nap.
6. Try starting again (from a different place, point of view, time, setting).
7. Rewrite what you wrote before.
8. Copy pages of someone else's writing. Especially a writer you adore.
9. Kick around your ideas with someone else, maybe someone who isn't a writer but is a good reader.
10. Get in a writing group.
11. Change your place of writing (get out of the house or stay at home — whichever you're not doing).
12. Change the time of your writing.
13. Change your clothes.
14. Set a deadline (a page a day, a scene by tomorrow, a rough draft by Tuesday).
15. Remove a deadline.
16. Use freewriting or stream of consciousness, or write nonsense.
17. Write your favorite words, then make sentences with them, then paragraphs.
18. Go to a poetry reading, just to listen.
19. Listen to music. Make music.
20. Go to a museum, a gallery. Look at art. Make art.
21. Read poetry aloud or listen to poetry or spoken-word CDs or stories.
22. Read a book you've been meaning to read. Reread a favorite.

> A problem with a piece of writing often clarifies itself if you go for a long walk.
>
> — HELEN DUNMORE

23. Take a long, literary breath. Write a single sentence for seven minutes or longer.

24. Write in your journal.

25. Meditate.

26. Go to the movies or rent or download a DVD. Create your own film festival of a favorite star or director or screenwriter or writer.

27. Work on another project (writing or otherwise).

28. Write a letter to someone describing your problem.

29. Let the piece cool off. Come back to it in a few weeks or months.

30. Notice the details. Look out your window and write what you see.

31. Start with one concrete detail and follow where it leads.

32. Plant some flowers. Work in the garden.

33. Light a candle, say a prayer, request a dream.

AUGUST 16	Write about smoke
AUGUST 17	You woke up and found him gone
AUGUST 18	On the front porch
AUGUST 19	You can have faith in _____
AUGUST 20	Write about the weight of sleep (after W. S. Merwin)

THE WRITING LIFE

WRITERS AND THEIR DAY JOBS

HANS CHRISTIAN ANDERSEN worked in a tobacco factory at age eleven.

JACK LONDON worked in a cannery at age thirteen.

CHARLES DICKENS pasted labels on bottles of shoe polish.

CARL SANDBURG was a firefighter, a traveling salesman, and secretary to the mayor of Milwaukee.

E. B. WHITE sold roach powder and played the piano.

> To support our work, most fiction writers inhabit the more menial and less glamorous regions of the literary economy. Usually there is a cubicle involved.
>
> ⌐ JAMES HYNES ⌐

ZANE GREY was a dentist.

WILLIAM CARLOS WILLIAMS was a doctor.

WALLACE STEVENS was a lawyer for an insurance company.

MONA SIMPSON worked as an ice cream scooper, a waitress, a stock clerk, a Christmas present wrapper, a neurophysiology lab assistant, a movie theater usher, an acupuncturist's assistant, and an editor.

ALICE MUNRO picked tobacco while a university student.

CARSON McCULLERS put in time as a waitress and played the piano for a dance class.

COLETTE supported herself by performing in a music hall, writing theater reviews, and, briefly, running a beauty salon.

CHRISTOPHER MARLOWE moonlighted as a counterespionage agent investigating English Catholics abroad.

ERICH MARIA REMARQUE sold tombstones and played the organ in an insane asylum.

RAYMOND CARVER's day job was a night job: he worked as a janitor.

MILAN KUNDERA worked as a laborer and a jazz musician.

DANIEL DEFOE was a spy and spin doctor for the Tories and the Whigs.

WILLIAM BURROUGHS was an anthropologist and a private investigator.

ISAAC ASIMOV compiled encyclopedias and taught chemistry.

CHRISTOPHER ISHERWOOD served as secretary to a violinist.

T. S. ELIOT was a banker.

PHILIP LARKIN was a librarian.

RUSSELL BANKS was a plumber.

MARK JACOBSON was a cabdriver.

RICHARD FARIÑA was a songwriter.

> If someone asks you what you do and you say, "I'm a writer," the next question will be, "But what do you do for a living?"
>
> ⌒ GEORGES BORCHARDT ⌒

MAY SARTON worked during the World War II years for the Office of War Information, where she wrote documentary film scripts.

WALT WHITMAN was a typesetter, a journalist, an itinerant schoolteacher, and a newspaper editor.

HERMAN MELVILLE was a customs inspector for the New York Harbor Authority.

ANTHONY TROLLOPE was a civil servant for the postal authority and is credited with inventing the letter box.

WILLIAM FAULKNER served as postmaster for the University of Mississippi post office.

HART CRANE was a factory worker in Cleveland.

ALEX HALEY spent twenty years in the U. S. Coast Guard.

MAYA ANGELOU worked as a cook and managed a restaurant.

Among others, E. L. DOCTOROW, MARY McCARTHY, TONI MORRISON, WILLIAM STYRON, GORE VIDAL, LISA ALTHER, JOHN ASHBERY, RICK MOODY, AMY CLAMPITT, and DOROTHY PARKER worked in publishing.

Most writers I know have a day job — tech writers, schoolteachers, massage therapists, accountants, web designers, tutors, librarians, lawyers, police officers, engineers. Most of us dream of the day we can be full-time writers. Meantime, we just keep showing up at the page, getting it down.

HUNTING AND GATHERING

Like our ancestors, writers go beyond the familiar and safe confines of home to gather those things that feed and clothe our work; no one will bring them to us. It's necessary and it's also a grand adventure.

Though it's possible to write wildly and imaginatively without ever leaving home (Emily Dickinson in her white room; Marcel Proust beneath his covers), most of us must go "out there" to experience the world, to interact with other people, to take our senses on a field trip; to watch, observe, record, and harvest. On each excursion we fill our sacks with booty, then haul it home and spill it out on our writer's workbench.

> You should use anything that improves the quality of your writing and doesn't get in the way of your story.
>
> ⌒ STEPHEN KING ⌒

Have some fun — go on hunting and gathering expeditions:

- Dress as your character and go out into the world as him or her. Observe and interact from his or her point of view.
- Imagine that this is the last time you will venture out: you are dying, you are going to prison, you are moving away, you are withdrawing.
- Notice everything that is dying and how it is dying; notice everything that is new and fresh.
- Pay attention to everything that is yellow or green or red.
- Pretend you cannot read or cannot understand the language.
- What if you are deaf? Blind? Cannot speak?
- Act as if this is the first time you've been to this place. You are a foreigner, a visitor.
- Note what is man-made and what is natural. Notice attractions and rejections, confluences.
- Go to the same place at the same time every day for a few weeks or a month. Record what is the same, what is different.

{*See also* Places to Practice, p. 68; Pay Attention, p. 29; Write from the Senses; p. 30}

IMAGES THAT HAUNT YOU

Close your eyes, and an image appears behind your darkened lids; write in your notebook, and your words take shape around the same familiar vision. It appears and reappears, sometimes shape-shifting, sometimes merely disguising itself. Explorations of this recurring image might lead to a single piece, or the idea could be symbolic of a major theme, the leitmotif of your writing.

"I think all writers have one thing that sticks with them, one sticking point, and they write their books over and over again until they've solved it," said Anne Rivers Siddons.

For many years my "sticking" thing was women and children — an old woman finds a newborn in a Dumpster, a mother leaves her baby on a train, a woman runs away from home with her three daughters. Story themes continued to appear in different forms, and I wrote them without knowing their significance. I don't write about women and children anymore. I don't know what it was, that particular knot in my psychic shoelace, but I believe my writing was teaching me something important or helping me to work through some issues on a deeper level.

My friend Dian writes about sisters, Michelle's theme is relationships gone awry, precocious children appear in many of Wendy's stories, and for James it's the adventurer on a quest.

Often, rather than a theme that surfaces, single images have haunted me until I wrote them. Stopped at a traffic light one afternoon, I spotted a woman high up on the balcony of a retirement home, watering plants. She wore a brilliant green dress, and her silver hair glinted in the sunlight. An image of her free-falling down the side of the building suddenly appeared to me and, for three years, the image would not leave me be — until finally I wrote the story. (In my story, she didn't fall to her death, but instead landed in the swimming pool and floated to the top looking for all the world like a water lily in full bloom.) Other recurrent visions have been homeless men shouting at the sky and cowgirls in leather fringe riding trick ponies. This last one still wants to be written.

> The thing that teases the mind over and over for years, and at last gets itself put down rightly on paper — whether little or great — it belongs to literature.
>
> ⌁ SARAH ORNE JEWETT ⌁

As an exercise, create a list of your recurring images, noting a few concrete details of each in a paragraph or so. For the next few practice sessions, expand on one of the pieces to see where it takes you.

> Certain images create private little excitements in the mind.
>
> ⮞ E. L. DOCTOROW ⮜

You can trust these recurring images. Their resonance signifies a deeper connection, perhaps something that can never be clearly stated, something outside the cognitive and beyond language, a conjuration from that mystical place of spirit. Writing these echoing images will reveal you to yourself. This is one of the gifts of writing.

{*See also* Turn the Soil, p. 92; Rereading Your Practice Pages, p. 185; Discover What You Want to Write About, p. 210}

AUGUST 21	The geography of home
AUGUST 22	You're packing a suitcase
AUGUST 23	The smell of air in winter
AUGUST 24	Write the place the landscape dissolves
AUGUST 25	In search of impossible light (after Larissa Szporluk)

WRITING ABOUT REAL PEOPLE

How will Aunt Thelma react when she reads what you wrote about her? Can your ex sue you for writing about his bad habits and bad breath? Writing about real people can be tricky; it can cause one set of problems as you write and a whole other set when the piece is published.

During the writing, you might be afraid to write about certain people because you're concerned you might hurt their feelings. You're scared you might reveal secrets or betray confidences. In this phase, the editor and censor are constantly on duty with their sharpened pencils and pursed lips, circling and pacing as you write. So you get stuck, or you write around something, or you hold back, and the writing suffers.

But let's say you circumvented or outwitted or somehow evaded the editor and the censor and wrote something true about real people, something they might look upon as harmful and mean-spirited. And let's say this material got published. The problems that might arise from this scenario have to do with libel, and both you and your publisher could end up in a court of law.

For most of us, the first situation is far more common than the second. Even better, there are several ways to combat the first problem, and most of them make the second problem moot.

> All good fiction is moral, in that it is imbued with the world, and powered by our real concerns: love, death, how-should-I-live.
>
> ⌒ GEORGE SAUNDERS ⌒

In writing fiction, one sure way to avoid the psychological tangles that come from the feeling that you're exposing people and telling secrets is to disguise the real person as somebody else, somebody totally fictional, made up of bits and pieces of other people — a composite character. Right away you're guaranteed more freedom to fictionalize, and, knowing how characters like to take over stories, there might be some surprising turns of event you would have never included if you'd tried to stick to the "way it happened" with the real person.

Another technique to sidestep the problem is to change enough facts that the real person would never recognize him- or herself. Make her a him, give him more children or take some away, move the family from Cleveland to Boise, have the character drive a bus instead of sell insurance. Truly fictionalize your fiction.

If you're writing nonfiction, you can get permission from those you're writing about. This is a gracious and perhaps smart thing to do. Annie Dillard said she wouldn't publish her memoir if someone in her family didn't want her to.

> It doesn't matter how "real" your story is, or how "made up": what matters is its necessity.
>
> ⬡ ANNE ENRIGHT ⬡

Another approach, most common among autobiographers and memoirists, is to change some of the names or biographical facts, alterations that are disclosed in a disclaimer at the beginning of the book, or in the introduction.

In the end, some people you write about, minor characters, perhaps, may experience hurt feelings and not suffer them well — Aunt Thelma, for example, may get her feelings hurt because you wrote about the time you got sick from her apple dumplings. As a writer, you have to take this chance and may have to pay this price. However, hurt feelings aren't libelous. To be libeled, a person must prove harm done and that, as a writer, you intended them harm. If you're concerned, check with a lawyer.

Remember this: if you have lived it, seen it, experienced it, or felt it, it's your story, and you have a right to tell your story any way you want.

{*See also* Family Stories, p. 161; Transferring Real Life to Fiction, p. 201; It's All Copy, p. 236}

AUGUST 26	The stranger at the crossroads
AUGUST 27	In anticipation of catastrophe
AUGUST 28	He called you by your real name
AUGUST 29	Write what is forbidden
AUGUST 30	Write what came first
AUGUST 31	They're talking in whispers

BEYOND PRACTICE

HOT NIGHTS/WILD WOMEN
(FOR MEN, TOO)

When was the last time you howled at the moon? Dallied in erotica? Wrote about your skin and bones and wild imaginings? This writing session says do it now. Do it when trees hang heavy with ripened peaches and heat shimmers the night sky. Do it when your writer's mind is restless and it's too hot to sleep. Surrender your pen to your outlaw self and write in the language of thunderstorms and sudden passion. Write in vibrant hues, the colors of the night — indigo, violet, the deepest shades of magenta. Put your ear to the ground and write its thrumming. Write your heartbeat, your blood song, the rattle and clack of your bones, the sizzle of air against skin. Write the geography of your soul, the map of your senses, the certain and electric poetry of your body. Write from your reckless mind and resonating memories.

> The poet's job is to find a name for everything: to be a fearless finder of the names of things.
>
> ⌒ JANE KENYON ⌒

This is what you do: Let loose your hair, your clothes. Unbind yourself. Go barefoot, go by yourself, go outside and into the night. Let the moon be full and an untamed scent be in the air. Breathe it deep into your lungs and feel it beating against your ribs, then let it out in a long, sustained howl. Offer yourself up to the moon and listen to the echo of your own yowling coyote song. You are wild woman, wild man, and according to Clarissa Pinkola Estés, "fluent in the language of dreams, passion, and poetry."

Under the night sky, beneath the moon of new ripening corn, the moon when cherries turn black, write in your notebook. Write fourteen fruits you love to eat and thirteen ways you like to eat them; list thirty-three ways you want to make love and twenty-five places you want to do it. Lie on your back in the grass and search out your own constellation in the sky. Say its myth. Sing and chant and dance to your own night music. Name yourself wild woman or man and write your real name. Do it as an act of liberation. Stay up all night long, watch the stars wheel across the heavens, track their path on the pages of your notebook. Describe the colors of the sky, write its depth. At the darkest hour, gather wood and build a fire. Listen for the dawn.

More suggested prompts:

- In the heat of the night
- This is where I come from
- Write about the full moon
- Write about a time you made love
- My body is . . .

{SEPTEMBER}

Follow your inner moonlight; don't hide the madness.
— ALLEN GINSBERG

WRITE SPECIFIC DETAILS

The specificity of detail is what brings your writing to life. However, writing specific details doesn't mean your writing has to be factually true. The truth isn't in the facts; it's in the details.

"The more detail that you give to the reader, the more you help their imagination," said National Book Award–winner Charles Johnson. It matters little what kind of sandwich you actually ordered during that lunch when your lover broke up with you, but if you say you were eating a grilled cheese or, for irony's sake, let's make it a hero or maybe turkey sandwich, the moment becomes more alive and real for the reader. They can taste that turkey and mayo on sourdough and how a mouthful of tears affects it. Rather than *bird*, write *sparrow* or *starling*; instead of *tree*, write *eucalyptus* or *willow*. Be specific with details that are true and right for the piece. But be careful not to bloom your azaleas in the fall or pop up your toast before Herbert Hoover was elected. Research, if you need to, for accuracy.

Of course, you can go overboard and use so many details that reading your piece feels like slogging through seaweed. Choose your details carefully; use the most telling ones. "I try to go for the detail that lights up in me like a neon light," said Spalding Gray.

Pay attention, not just when you're writing, but as you go through your days and nights. Notice what you notice — especially through your five senses — and write it down.

TIP OF THE MONTH

Make small things big. If a very slight detail — a gesture, a remark, or a glance — is extremely poignant, make something of it. Wrap a scene around it.

— JOHN BERENDT

SEPTEMBER 1	"Even the lightning spoke well of them" (after W. S. Merwin)	
SEPTEMBER 2	He (she) asked you to dance	
SEPTEMBER 3	Write what was broken	
SEPTEMBER 4	We go out after dark	
SEPTEMBER 5	Write about dispelling loneliness	

FAMILY STORIES

Everyone has family stories. In many ways they are all the same, yet they are all different. "I could write a book about my crazy family," people say. And indeed, most of us could. Flannery O'Connor said that if we survived childhood we have enough material to last a lifetime.

Family stories in and of themselves — the blow-by-blow of what happened to whom — are not often the stuff of great literature, but that doesn't mean they shouldn't be written. Many people choose to write a family history or autobiography just to share it with the family. Others use family stories as a way into memoir or personal narrative essays, even (or maybe most often) as the spark to start fictional fires. Writing family stories does more than recollect times gone by: it celebrates what is grand and grieves what needs to be grieved; it is one of the ways we heal. Whether you want to write your autobiography or simply use your family memories as grist for your writer's mill, here are some exercises that can help you harvest stories rich with detail, and find the truth.

> Anyone at any age is able to tell the story of his or her life with authority.
>
> ⮑ E. L. DOCTOROW ⮐

- Use the "I remember..." exercise described on page 231. Begin with "I remember my mother..." or "I remember my father..." or use the name of another family member.
- As suggested by poet Steve Kowit in his book *In the Palm of Your Hand*, begin with a date such as "Summer, 19__," and write a memory, then list another date, and so on; or begin with the phrase "The year I turned eight," "The year I turned sixteen," and so on. Be sure to use the same intuitive, spontaneous writing that you used in the "I remember..." exercises.
- Sketch a floor plan of the house you grew up in, then write about each of the rooms. As you describe them, bring forth memories of being in those rooms, alone and with other family members. Remember to use specific details, drawing on your sense memories.
- Create a map of your childhood neighborhood. Write what it was like in the spring or winter, or at eight o'clock in the morning or

three in the afternoon. At night. Write the trees and the houses, the streets and fences. Look in your neighbor's windows.

- Write about holidays. Family gatherings, special occasions. Remember your birthdays and how they were celebrated. Sit everyone down at the dinner table and re-create a meal together.
- Do character sketches of members of your family. Freewrite for ten or twelve minutes. Go beyond physical characteristics and include attitudes, beliefs, habits and quirks, manner of speech, maybe some dialogue. Include the three aspects of any character: physical, psychological, and social. Use lines like "Uncle George was the kind of man who...," then list four or five attributes.
- Imagine you're watching your mother. Write what you see.
- List some habits of your father.
- Write about comings and goings. Who left, who stayed.
- Make a list of the smells of your grandmother's bedroom, your parents' car, the back porch. List the sounds you heard in the morning when you awoke, and what kept you awake at night. List the tastes that came from the staples of family meals (I remember a wedge of iceberg lettuce served with a dollop of mayonnaise; chocolate chip cookies wrapped in waxed paper and stuffed inside brown paper lunch bags). Remember textures: the shag carpeting in the family room, your father's favorite sweater, the soft fur of the puppy's ear. Note these fragments of sense memories as quickly as you can, without stopping to think. Items from your lists can serve as laden prompts for subsequent writing sessions. Each sense memory is a door into a specific time and place that holds a family story.
- Write a collection of firsts: first day of school, first date, first kiss, first time you saw blood, first funeral, first book you read, first time you thought differently than your mother or father, first time you were scared.

> I find a little something that I exaggerate, a little; gradually I have the autobiography on its way to becoming a lie. The lie, of course, is more interesting.
>
> ⌒ JOHN IRVING ⌒

- In your mind's eye, create a photograph of your family posed together. Notice who's leaning into whom, who's touching, where hands are placed and eyes are focused. Look into the faces; write what you see. Write what happens right after the photo is snapped.

{*See also* Transferring Real Life to Fiction, p. 201; Writing about Real People, p. 155}

CLICHÉS AND OTHER BAD HABITS

Clichés, like petty crimes and faux pas, are often committed without thought. "First thought is best in Art, second in other matters," said William Blake. So the "first thought, best thought" dictum that works so well in evoking images and memories may not be the best source when it comes to word choice and creative phrasing. Either out of simple laziness or faster-than-light efficiency, when asked to "complete this phrase," often the brain's best shot will be something tired and mundane. For example, just off the top of your head (there's a cliché for you), complete these phrases with your first thought:

> A cliché is like a coin that has been handled too much. Once language has been overly handled, it no longer leaves a clear imprint.
>
> ⌒ JANET FITCH ⌒

Soft as _____.
Dark as _____.
The clouds were like _____.
Hot as _____.
_____ as rocks.

You get the point.

What's a cliché? In talking to her advanced writing group, Janet Fitch repeated to us what her teacher, Kate Braverman, said to her: "For you, it's anything you've ever seen or heard before." Now try describing a mountain range or an ice cream cone.

Clichés aren't just hackneyed phrases or descriptions. Characters, situations, plots, settings can also be clichéd — the ways you can be banal are as common as _____. (What was your first thought? Mine was *houseflies*.)

Every writer commits clichés. One of the jobs of rewriting is to find these gravy stains on your literary necktie and clean them up. Also, the more aware you are of clichés, the less likely you are to use them. Here are a few tips to circumnavigate, levitate above, tunnel under, ride roughshod over, and generally avoid these bad habits.

- Read your writing aloud after every draft. Clichés stand out more clearly when they're spoken. The undiscerning eye sometimes sides with the lazy brain.

- Go through and underline each suspect in a different ink color. Notice the frequency of usage. The more brightly colored your page, the more work you have to do.

- Ask your writing partner to give you feedback. If your group hands out manuscripts for read-and-critique, have the readers mark clichés with a big "CL."

- Don't settle for the first phrase you come up with; close your eyes and try to see the image more clearly. Write and rewrite.

- Just like with real people, the more you get to know your characters, the more individualistic they'll become. Ask them questions, go deeper, find what's unique about each one and develop it.

- Look for telling details in people, places, and things; bypass the general for the specific.

> What I like to do is treat words as a craftsman does his wood or stone...to hew, carve, mould, coil, polish, and plane them into patterns, sequences, sculptures, figures of sound expressing some lyrical impulse.
>
> ⮑ DYLAN THOMAS ⮐

- Have commonplace events take place in uncommon settings. Turn that around and make uncommon events happen in ordinary settings.

- Become cliché conscious. Note their appearance in everything you read. As with a wary parent of teenagers after curfew, the more alert you become, the less likely they'll be to sneak in unnoticed.

As the old saying goes, "avoid clichés like the plague."

{*See also* Auditioning Words, p. 32; About Language, p. 48; Better Verbs, Fewer Adverbs, p. 134; Wordplay, p. 202; When the Words Aren't Working: A Helping Hand, p. 169}

STREAM OF CONSCIOUSNESS AND OTHER INTUITIVE WRITING

What a great freedom to write stream of consciousness, to let the pen fly like a dervish while you hang on for the ride, nabbing thoughts as they appear out of some wild, flamboyant place in your mind. Stream of consciousness and other intuitive writing is the magic carpet of writing techniques, producing funny, fantastic, surreal stuff, spoken in a language rich with imagery and musicality.

Called by many names — stream of consciousness, free-intuitive writing, flow writing, free association, automatic writing, spontaneous writing — this method of writing reaches into the deep recesses of the intuitive and brings forth words and ideas that can surprise and delight you. Use it to unearth new images and ideas, to unstick yourself, to set a rhythm, to free your imagination, and, sometimes, just for the fun of it.

It's a simple technique, calling for nothing more than emptying your mind, then hopping on the back of any passing thought or image and riding it to the next, and then the next. André Breton, leader of the surrealist movement in Paris in the 1920s, suggested this: "Attain the most passive or receptive state of mind possible. Forget your genius, your talents, and those of everyone else. . . . Write quickly with no preconceived subject, so quickly that you retain nothing and are not tempted to reread. Continue as long as you please."

> Language haunts my sleep; phrases bubble up through my dreams.
>
> ⮑ WILLIAM LASHNER ⮐

When you use stream of consciousness writing, don't expect any logical sequence of thought. But do expect surprises. This technique delves into the innermost places of your subconscious; it can reveal thoughts, motivations, and desires. When images appear and reappear, the intuitive is giving you information. Pay attention.

THE WRITING LIFE

QUIRKS AND IDIOSYNCRASIES

WILLIAM FAULKNER outlined the plot of *A Fable* on the walls of his office. His wife had the text painted over. Enraged, Faulkner rewrote it and shellacked the wall. You can still see it at his home in Oxford, Mississippi.

GUSTAVE FLAUBERT kept his lover's slippers and mittens in his desk drawer.

ALEXANDRE DUMAS ate an apple at seven each morning under the Arc de Triomphe.

BHARATI MUKHERJEE will not leave the house if someone sneezes just as she's getting ready to leave, and she doesn't cut her nails on certain days of the week.

> Writing is a socially acceptable form of schizophrenia.
>
> E. L. DOCTOROW

ANNE RIVERS SIDDONS's husband reports that she makes a nest of papers, like a mouse getting ready for winter, then she starts walking into walls just before she begins a new novel.

Every time **ALICE HOFFMAN** starts a new book, she paints her office a different color, one that resonates with the book's theme.

STEPHEN KING goes through these motions when he sits down to write: "I have a glass of water or I have a cup of tea. I have my vitamin pill; I have my music; I have my same seat; and the papers are all arranged in the same places."

GERTRUDE STEIN scribbled her poems on odd scraps of paper in her Ford, named "Godiva," parked at the curb. She had discovered that her lofty position in the driver's seat was an inspiring spot in which to write.

HENRY DAVID THOREAU talked with forest animals. "I talked to [the woodchuck] in quasi forest lingo, baby talk, at any rate in a conciliatory tone, and thought that I had some influence on him."

As a child, **LOUISA MAY ALCOTT** wrote passionate letters to **RALPH WALDO EMERSON**, but she never sent them. She sat in the tall walnut tree in front of his house at midnight, singing to the moon.

CHARLES DICKENS walked twenty to thirty miles a day. He also placed objects on his desk in exactly the same position, always oriented his bed north-south, and touched certain objects three times for luck.

HANS CHRISTIAN ANDERSEN put a sign next to his bed that read I AM NOT REALLY DEAD.

SAINT-POL-ROUX hung the inscription THE POET IS WORKING from his door while he slept.

EMILY DICKINSON wouldn't see her dressmaker, go out of the house, or expose her handwriting. Her sister addressed all her letters.

Five years after *Nightwood* was published, **DJUNA BARNES** left Paris, gave up smoking and drinking, refused interviews and photographs, and removed all the mirrors from her apartment.

SHIRLEY JACKSON owned more than five hundred books on witchcraft.

At his funeral, **LANGSTON HUGHES** had arranged for a jazz trio to play "Do Nothing Till You Hear From Me."

And a few citings of sartorial eccentricities:

EDGAR ALLAN POE always wore black; **EMILY DICKINSON**, only white; **MARK TWAIN** also attired himself in white, with shirts he personally designed that buttoned down the back. **CARL SANDBURG** sported a green eye-shade when he worked, and **E. B. WHITE** tied on a surgical mask in public to protect himself from contagious diseases. **JOHN CHEEVER** donned his only suit of clothes when he went to his studio in the morning. He hung it up while he worked in his underwear, then dressed and returned home. **ALLAN GURGANUS** said he wears a professional mover's zip-up uniform because "I perspire so freely that I sweat my way through the fiction." **FORREST McDONALD** was said to write history on his rural Alabama porch — naked.

> Writing a book is not polite. It's absorbing and anti-social.
>
> ⮌ PIA Z. EHRHARDT ⮌

WHEN THE WORDS AREN'T WORKING:
A HELPING HAND

You're going to have days like this: you reread your writing and discover you've used the same word three different times in the same paragraph. And it's not even a good word. It's a boring, mundane word. Worse, the only verb that attempts any movement at all is something past tense and lethargic: *was*. A snail of a word, taupe and gray in the middle of your sidewalk of a sentence.

You need help.

On days like this you can be thankful to Webster and Roget and others like them who made dictionaries and thesauri. These generous, helpful books can be your inspirations and your guides. They can show you the way to words you forgot and words you never knew existed. Get big, jumbo-sized reference books and keep them within easy reach. Bookmark your online favorites. You can be inspired just watching visual thesauri as words weave and web across the screen. Discover language books or sites that give you the origins of words and phrases. Dive into them just for the fun of it. Liven up your writing and increase your vocabulary at the same time.

> You most likely need a thesaurus, a rudimentary grammar book, and a grip on reality.
>
> ⌒ MARGARET ATWOOD ⌒

I once worked for an editor who would not abide the use of a thesaurus. "If you don't know the word, you can't use it," he growled. But, oh, how I love my Roget's. Late at night, when the candle flickers and I'm hanging on by my teeth to meet a morning deadline, and I give my manuscript one last edit, only to discover I have used the word *gift* four times on one page, how grateful I am for my thesaurus when I can look up *gift* and find *present*, *favor*, *legacy*, *bounty*, *offering*, *blessing*, and nearly forty other synonyms that my weary brain could not locate in its own online dictionary.

At a weekly read-and-critique session, one writer makes a list of all the words she hears that she doesn't know. When she gets home, she looks them up in her dictionary and tries to use them in her writing practice sometime during the next week. Others do this as they read, always keeping pen and paper nearby.

You can create your own stash of words in your notebook, too, as well as add words to the custom dictionary you build as you write on your computer. This dictionary doesn't provide definitions, but once you've added a particular word to your custom dictionary, the spell-checker won't continue to flag it.

{*See also* Wordplay, p. 202; Better Verbs, Fewer Adverbs, p. 134; About Language, p. 48; Writer's Notebooks, p. 19; Auditioning Words, p. 32}

SEPTEMBER 11	"The bittersweet autumn of the body" (after May Sarton)
SEPTEMBER 12	Write about going underground
SEPTEMBER 13	She left a note
SEPTEMBER 14	A collection of lies
SEPTEMBER 15	"Houses have their secrets" (after Yannis Ritsos)

PRACTICE ACCOUTREMENTS

Though some say the best view for writers is a blank wall — that is, the less outside stimulation, the better — others believe in seducing the Muse with evocative accessories. Each writer gets to find his or her own way, and whatever works is good. After all, Schiller had his rotten apples. If you're one who likes to arouse the creative with embellishments, following are some accoutrements other writers have brought into play.

- **Music:** Especially the classics — Mozart, Chopin, Haydn — but jazz, too, or world music, or ambient. Rock and roll if you've got the stamina, and blues if that's what it takes. I've also used recordings of thunderstorms, the ocean, night sounds, crickets, and songbirds.

- **Scents and Aromas:** With so many aromatherapy scents to choose from, you can create a cacophony of odoriferous atmospheres. Think, too, of natural scents: a bowl of oranges, fresh rosemary, sprigs of pine or eucalyptus, bouquets of flowers. Wear your character's signature cologne as you write. Light incense, brew coffee, burn sage.

- **Photographs and Postcards:** Whether they remind you of the place you're writing or are simply stimulating to look at, photographs stir the creative. Look beyond what you see for the smell and feel of the place or the people. (Great places to hunt down old photography and art books are used bookstores or thrift stores.)

> I never sit down to write without music playing in the background. It opens me up. It thrills me. It sets me afire with rhythm and joy.
>
> ⁐ T. C. BOYLE ⁐

- **Poetry:** Read some poetry before you begin writing, or listen to spoken-word or poetry CDs or podcasts. Take a break from your writing and read a few poems or use a line or image from a poem to write from.

- **Objects:** Bring objects to your practice session — a seashell to explore and name, an amethyst with its miniature purple mountain range, a fan from Bali, weeds from the garden, snail shells, locust carcasses, gumdrops, BBs, buttons, postage stamps. Make a collection of objects that you store in a basket on a shelf. Reach into it and surprise yourself.

- **Clothing:** Dress as your character, dress as the opposite gender, wear someone else's clothes, slip into something you would never normally wear: a feather boa, a flowered housedress, wedgies or cowboy boots, spikey strappy sandals. Work in your pajamas, your underwear, silk lingerie.

{*See also* The Writing Life: Invoking the Muse, p. 37; Saying Yes to the Muse, p. 110; How to Create a Space of Your Own, p. 17}

> The point isn't to believe in hokum, but to turn yourself over to the force of ritual, to deliver the project out of your own neurotic proprietorship.
>
> ⮑ JONATHAN LETHEM ⮐

SEPTEMBER 16	Write about fever dreams
SEPTEMBER 17	Write what gets under the skin
SEPTEMBER 18	The landscape of longing
SEPTEMBER 19	"After we became acquainted"
SEPTEMBER 20	"There are some questions one should know by heart" (after Henri Coulette)

FIND YOUR TRIBE:
WHY HANG OUT WITH OTHER WRITERS

Unlike your family and some of your friends, other writers don't think it odd that you talk about your characters as if they were actually alive. Other writers understand why you stay up half the night hunched over your computer, muttering to yourself. They know about the elusiveness of language, endings that won't come; they recognize the restlessness that comes with getting stuck in plot breakdowns. They also know the exhilaration of completing a chapter, a poem, or a short story because they experience it, too.

Hanging out with other writers is more than talking shop. It's different from a couple of fans sharing a beer and a game. Writers have always

> The great use of the workshop is that it teaches you to be a good, close reader.
>
> ⌒ TOBIAS WOLFF ⌒

sought the company of other writers; there is a hunger for a connection that goes beyond the jargon and lingo and gossip of the trade. Call it psychic, if you will, some kind of energy that vibrates at a sympathetic rate, something tribal and deep.

"[Writing's] a solitary act, and you need a community of like-minded souls to survive and to flourish," said Poet Laureate Stanley Kunitz. We are a species that gathers into community, not just we the writer species, but we the human species. Within these communities, we look for others who are like us. We form subcommunities and sub-subcommunities. When we are our best, we are inclusive and open. At our worst — when we operate out of fear — we become exclusive and protectionist. Ideally we are looking for both safety and freedom. The freedom to be who we are without pretensions or alibis, and the feeling of being safe in expressing who we are.

As a writer, when you're with your own kind, your writing is taken seriously, there is respect for the work that goes unspoken; no need for explaining or proving yourself. Within this circle there is an understanding that writing isn't about being published or making money or becoming famous; no need to justify how much time you spend on a piece of work that may never see print.

Julia Cameron said that creativity is a tribal experience and that "tribal elders will initiate the gifted youngsters who cross their path." Isn't it true that writers help one another? "Try this publication," they'll say, or, "Sure, I'll be glad to give your story a read through." I never would have found the courage to begin this book or the stamina to see it through to completion were it not for the generosity and enormous support of my writer friends.

> Find out what keeps you happy, motivated and creative.
>
> ⌒ A. L. KENNEDY ⌒

Of course, this connection doesn't happen among all writers. No matter what tribe you belong to, there will always be some members that just fry your banana. Even this you can use in your writing. But those close connections with your own kind, this is what home feels like. Find them and nurture them. It's crucial to your writerly health and well-being. It's soul food.

{*See also* How to Start a Writing Practice Group, p. 223; Find Support for Your Writing Life, p. 234}

SEPTEMBER 21	Write the language of fire
SEPTEMBER 22	The towns you drive through on the way to somewhere else
SEPTEMBER 23	We kept it in the basement
SEPTEMBER 24	Driving a rented truck
SEPTEMBER 25	What I said was not what I was thinking

HOW TO TELL WHEN THE CENSOR IS PRESENT

The censor is a completely different species from the critic or editor. The censor is that mean-spirited, tight-lipped, righteous character with a shriveled soul who hangs out on your extreme right. The censor is afraid of everything but disguises its fear by pronouncing judgments. Crossed-out words; cramped, crabby little handwriting; and bland, noncommittal verbiage all smell like the censor, musty and vaguely rancid. Here's a list of warning signs that the censor may be influencing your writing:

> Ultimately every writer must choose between safety and invention.
>
> ⌒ ALLEGRA GOODMAN ⌒

- Rejecting the "first thought, best thought" image if it feels risky
- Listening to the "you can't write *that*" commentary in your head
- Worrying that you might hurt someone
- Wondering what "they" will think of you
- Looking around to see if anyone is watching you write
- Writing dialogue that is boring, with characters who sound like polite company
- Crossing out dangerous words, replacing them with safer words
- Avoiding writing certain scenes or memories
- Using vague, generalized, or trite descriptions that keep the real stuff at a distance rather than concrete, vivid, original writing that tells the truth
- Stopping suddenly and taking another, safer track, or quitting altogether
- Drifting into ambiguity
- Feeling embarrassed as you write or upon rereading
- Choosing not to read your writing aloud
- Immediately closing your notebook after you've finished
- Feeling guilty or ashamed, as if you've done something wrong or bad

- Leaving the group right after it's over and not returning to the group after a particularly vulnerable session
- Abandoning your writing completely for periods of time

Try as I might, there's nothing good I can find to say about the censor. If I had my way, I would pair up censorship with perfectionism and send them off hand in flinty hand to the boneyard.

{*See also* Avoiding the Truth, p. 98; How to Tell When the Critic Is Present, p. 90; Take Risks, p. 132}

SEPTEMBER 26	Write about taking a shower	
SEPTEMBER 27	"When loneliness comes stalking"	
	(after Mary Oliver)	
SEPTEMBER 28	Write about denial	
SEPTEMBER 29	The way water feels on skin	
SEPTEMBER 30	Peeling an orange	

WHEN YOUR WRITING EMBARRASSES YOU

I know a woman who, when she was twenty-five, burned everything she'd ever written — and she'd been writing half her life. Seeing herself so exposed on the page made her too uncomfortable; she was unable to separate herself at twenty-five from the passionate, angst-ridden fifteen-year-old whose writing was clumsy and naive. Or the eighteen-year-old who composed rhyming, sentimental poetry. She thought her writing was herself.

Sometimes in writing practice, you will lose yourself to the page and you won't be conscious of what you are writing. When you finish, you may feel as if you have been transported to another place and time, and maybe you have been. Reading what you've written may embarrass you because it reveals and exposes you, because it's so bad or because it's so unfalteringly good, because you wrote about your wildness and damaged the paper with all that raw energy.

"The best writers reveal something about themselves that a smarter person would choose to hide," said writer and editor Ken Foster.

Remember this: Your writing is not you. It is an expression of you that sometimes comes from a deep, unconscious place. And just as from time to time you have thoughts you cannot believe came from your mind — tearing the tongue from a sassy two-year-old, for example, or ravishing a stranger in a restaurant — what you write may be shocking, surprising, or downright embarrassing. "That

> Putting pen to paper, fingers to keyboard, is always a risk, as the writer well knows.
>
> ⬱ JAYNE ANNE PHILLIPS ⬱

came from me?" you say, incredulous. This is when you reach into your tool belt and pull out your sense of humor. When a shrug of self-acceptance rolls your shoulders and you shake your head at your wild mind and audacious imagination.

To be a writer is to be vulnerable to your art; to be a courageous writer is to do it anyway.

{*See also* Being Vulnerable on the Page, p. 123; Take Risks, p. 132; How to Tell When the Censor Is Present, p. 175; "If You Want to Write" (especially no. 6), p. 131}

BEYOND PRACTICE

WRITING MARATHON

I first read about writing marathons in Natalie Goldberg's book *Writing Down the Bones*. Over the years, I've staged many a marathon — from four to twelve hours or more. Seasonal marathons and pre-holiday marathons, late-night marathons and pizza party marathons, happy hour marathons, write in the New Year marathons, and the record-setting Blazing Typewriters Fundraising Marathon which, with the advancement of technology, has morphed into the annual Blazing Laptops Write-a-Thon.

Marathons are not a test of creative endurance. They are a way to immerse yourself in your writing, to tread new ground, experiment, explore, take some chances, maybe break through barriers and let the words fall where they may.

Make your marathon as long as you want — half a day to all night long. Experience shows that half a day leaves writers wanting more and beyond twelve hours wears them out and makes them more than a little wonky. But wonky can be good.

> The mysterious energy required to turn silence into words and roll those words perpetually uphill originates deep within the soul.
>
> ⌒ WALTER KIRN ⌒

Here's how it works: Gather together a bevy of writers, five to fifteen, for a set amount of time. Create a comfortable writing space. Provide all the prompts yourself or invite each writer to bring a prompt. Working with a variety of topics and accoutrements will keep the proceedings lively. Use the same guidelines for your marathon that you use for writing practice.

Following are some of the prompts I have found to be effective:

- collections of commonplace items that writers can choose from
- color themes such as everything in red, or "going for the gold"
- postcards, some of places and another set with photos of people for whom monologues are created
- photographs cut from books

- maps
- small, decorative boxes that contain even smaller items
- sensory prompts that can be smelled, tasted, touched, or listened to
- music
- jewelry
- personal items (participants remove something they're wearing and put it in the center of the table)

Also effective are interactive prompts that participants help create. For example, everyone writes a secret on a slip of paper, folds it, and tosses it in the prompt basket. Or one person writes the first name of a character; the next writes a last name; the third, a telling detail; and the fourth writes a monologue for this character. Use a book of writing exercises or prompts (such as this one).

I generally open with an inspirational reading or a poem that sets the tone and sometimes a "throw anything on the page" quick-write as a warm-up to get centered into the time and space. Begin with seven- or ten-minute sessions; work up to fifteen or eighteen, even thirty; then back down again. Invite readings after each writing, though with a large group not everyone will be able to read each time. Take breaks every one and a half to two hours.

Other tips: Provide nibbles and snacks, like fresh veggies and fruit. Of course, most marathoners I know like to lay on the sweets, too. Red licorice has been a surprising hit. Include plenty of water and a meal break if your session lasts more than half a day.

After a marathon, writers will probably be a little off balance. Spending even four hours in that deeper, intuitive space that writing leads to can leave us on another plane. Grounding exercises and physical reentry of some kind can help rebalance participants. Expect dreams.

Some prompts, just in case you need them:

- This is what my bones kept saying
- She was the kind of woman who . . .

- Write about a progression of events
- I live in _____
- Write about Saturday night
- These are the things you can trust
- Write about a small disappointment
- Skin

{ OCTOBER }

Writing is the axe that breaks the frozen sea within us.
— FRANZ KAFKA

WRITE WHAT MATTERS

If you don't care about what you're writing, neither will your readers. This doesn't mean you should take on only big subjects — war, peace, love, hunger, oppression. It means that if what matters to you is the way the light falls on the bougainvillea in the morning, that's what you should write about. If what matters to you is the relationship between sisters and brothers, then that's what you write about.

Write about what interests you, what you don't understand, what you want to learn more about. Amy Tan said, "I write about it [mothers and daughters] because I don't understand it, because it is such a mystery to me. If it ceases to be a mystery, and if I were an expert on it, I wouldn't write about it. I like to write about things that bother me in some way, that I have a lot of conflict with."

Reread your writing to discover recurring themes and images. Look for hints and innuendos within spontaneous or stream of consciousness writings. If you're bored with what you're writing, or lackadaisical about your commitment, return to the idea that birthed it. More than one writer has been drawn off track by comments from her writing group or misdirection from a friend. "Let nobody, your mother, your grandmother, your agent, your publisher, your producer, nobody tell you the creator what you should do," said Alex Haley, who invested twelve years in writing *Roots*, his life-changing book.

Be a passionate writer.

TIP OF THE MONTH

Your obligation as an editor, for yourself or for another, is to carefully select details that both mean the most and are the most authentic.

— SUSAN BELL

{
OCTOBER	**1**	"The slow combinations of the night" (after David St. John)
OCTOBER	**2**	What was forgotten
OCTOBER	**3**	The scent of ocean fog
OCTOBER	**4**	Write about unsubstantiated rumors
OCTOBER	**5**	Soaking in a tub
}

WHAT DO I DO WITH
ALL THESE PAGES?

Once you start writing on a daily basis, the pages will pile up. You'll fill notebook after notebook with bits and pieces from practice sessions. What do you do with all this writing?

You may feel it's just practice, not worth saving, and set your notebooks out at the curb every Tuesday for recycling.

On the other hand, you may want to save every sentence, every paragraph, every practice session, even if you never look at the notebooks again. (Let your biographers have a fling with them when you're old and famous.)

Writers who use the practice sessions for filling in stories, novels, or essays may take one day a week to keyboard all the handwritten entries into the computer for editing and may not want to keep the notebooks after that.

Some may want to reread the entries once a month and tag those pieces for transplanting that might take root in a different setting. Gina Cameron says her notebooks live on the top shelf of her study where "my characters conspire and think up tales for the next time my pen hits the page." Ellen Yaffa and Judy Geraci, both members of my Thursday Writers group, report that they revisit theirs from time to time to look for threads that can be reworked or woven together differently or to pull stories out of them.

> You write to discover what you want to say. You rewrite to discover what you have said and then rewrite to make it clear to other people.
>
> ⟜ DONALD MURRAY ⟜

One writer kept all her practice notebooks for a year, then packed them up in boxes and took them with her on a monthlong retreat to find out what she'd written. (Remember, writing practice shows you what you want to write about; themes emerge from disparate and seemingly disconnected pieces.)

Sometimes, upon rereading, you'll find a topic that will spark you to write again, maybe even a continuation of the original piece. (Topics can be recycled; it's almost guaranteed that you'll write something different each time.)

In *Writing Down the Bones*, Natalie Goldberg said she considered building a solar house out of her old notebooks. At that time, she had a stack about five feet high. I know another writer who plants a tree each Arbor Day as a symbolic gesture to acknowledge all the paper she's used during the course of that year's writing practice. You may want to do the same, creating a ceremony and celebration with some writing friends as a way of honoring the planet and giving back. (Imagine in some few years, another writer sitting in the shade of the tree you planted, leaning against its sturdy trunk, writing in her notebook.)

What you do with all your notebooks may depend on how often you move and whether or not you want to lug all those boxes around. Also, how much spare room you have in your current living space and whether you're basically a saver or a chucker. One thing's certain: your filled notebooks are a testament to your commitment to writing and the time you've invested in your craft. So whatever you ultimately do with those old notebooks, acknowledge yourself for that.

REREADING YOUR PRACTICE PAGES

Rereading your practice notebooks after a period of time is like taking a trip to a place that is at once familiar and yet somehow different, like revisiting an old neighborhood. Some streets and buildings you'll remember exactly, but when did that house with the dormer windows get built, and was that fence always leaning that way, ragged and a little dangerous? You may not remember how green this place was, how generous the trees.

Set aside an open-ended chunk of time; you won't want to rush the process. Gather several old notebooks, colored pens, and sticky notes and find a quiet place where you can lose yourself in the folds of your writing. It's best to read the notebooks in chronological order — there will be a natural building of pieces over time and recurrent writings, an organic unfurling of images; characters will reveal themselves over several sessions. You'll discover repeating themes and images, ideas tugging at your sleeve saying, *Write me, write me.*

> Our minds create narrative wholes from fragments because that story is necessary for us to go on living.
>
> ◄ SIRI HUSTVEDT ►

As you read, tag pieces for transplanting into other gardens. Use colored pens to mark recurring themes. Transcribe lines, images, and descriptions to a "keepers" notebook or similar computer file lest they be lost to the pages of these practice notebooks. You may also find pieces that you want to continue in subsequent practice sessions or topics to write about again. Make notes of all this. At the end of a rereading, your notebooks will look ragtag and earmarked and flapping like a ticker-tape parade.

Without a doubt you will find junk, pages and pages of junk. You may find yourself yawning over pieces that bored you even when you wrote them. But you'll also find jewels you didn't know existed, traces of your brilliance scrawled on practice pages and gleaming there beneath the oblique light of slightly detached vision that can come only with time and distance.

MAPPING THE PAGE

Maps show us where we are, or how to get where we're going. Maps are short-hand for written directions, a picture of a narrative that can go on and on:

> We remember in detail, we recognize in detail, we identify, we recreate.
>
> ⌐ FRANCINE PROSE ⌐

Turn left at the green building, or is it right? Anyhow, go about another mile or so, watch for a Worms for Sale sign just before you come to a sharp dogleg.... Mapping the pages of our work can give us direction, too. A visual diagram of our use of language, grammar, syntax, and a whole lot more. Get a handful of bright highlighters and create the topography of your writing.

- Use different colors for each use of a sense. Blue for sight, green for sound, pink for taste, and so on. After you've marked up a page, you can easily see which sense you rely on, which you need more of, and where you've gobbed so many together that the reader (and the characters) will experience sensory overload.

- Create a map of feeling or emotion words: *angry, happy, tired, hungry, glad,* and so on. This map will tell you when you need to go back for another pass at "show, don't tell."

- Mark your periods. A quick scan will indicate whether you've used a variety of sentence lengths.

- Highlight names. Do you use the characters' names too frequently? Or *I*?

- Look for adjectives and adverbs. "Adjectives and adverbs are rich and good and fattening," said Ursula LeGuin. "The main thing is not to overindulge." Regarding adverbs (the *-ly* words), I've heard every writer is allotted only five adverbs in a lifetime. We'd better use them wisely.

- Other mappable territory: passive language (mark the deserts of *was*es, the dead seas of *to be* verbs). Be on the lookout for those swampy qualifying words (*very, sort of, always, really*).

{*See also* A Few Sentences on the Sentence, p. 51; Show, Don't Tell, p. 78}

WHEN CHARACTERS APPEAR

Don't be surprised when characters, whom you could never in a million years think up, choose to make an appearance in your writing practice notebook. Welcome them. Invite them back. Give them plenty of space to tell their story. Use the daily prompts to write from their point of view. This is how stories and novels are born.

For example, if Tuesday's prompt is "Write a motel story," and some redheaded woman named Ruby shows up and wants to talk, listen to her. Next day, no matter what the prompt, let Ruby tell it. Give her enough elbow room, and she's bound to include some other characters. Invite them in, too; follow Ruby's lead and let the story and relationships unfold. Check in again the following day and see what these characters have been up to. Just start the writing with the daily prompt or begin with something that appeared the day before that interests you. Keep writing, and after a while you'll have some bones that you can cleave a story to. "The time will come when your characters will write your stories for you," said Ray Bradbury, "when your emotions, free of literary cant and commercial bias, will blast the page and tell the truth."

> There is something intensely interesting to me about characters getting swept into unexpected appetites, of not knowing they were going to do these things.
>
> — JOAN SILBER

Not every character who materializes through your writing practice is someone you'll want to stay with. They may be around for a while, then the story will fizzle out on its own; you'll get bored or they will, and the affair will end. You may never hear from them again or, at some later session, they may reappear. "All writers have a cast of characters that keep turning up under different names and different sexes," said Doris Lessing. "Sometimes these characters can surprise you; sometimes they go past so fast you often don't notice them."

Others won't leave you alone. My friend Amy Wallen's protagonist showed up at a writing marathon in 1997 and, several years and many practice sessions and rewrites later, made her public debut in 2006 in Amy's novel, *MoonPies and Movie Stars*.

Working with characters is like dancing: sometimes you lead, and sometimes they do. It's a matter of trusting your partner and listening to the music.

{*See also* Use Practice as Building Blocks, p. 126}

{
OCTOBER 11   "The secret history of anger" (after Ilya Kaminsky)

OCTOBER 12   She kept it in a box under the stairs

OCTOBER 13   Write what came first

OCTOBER 14   Something you inherited from your mother

OCTOBER 15   The names I've been called
}

THE WRITING LIFE

QUOTAS AND OTHER FACTS AND FIGURES

THOMAS MANN, working full time, wrote a page a day. He wrote every day.

For twenty-five years, **GUSTAVE FLAUBERT** finished a big book every five to seven years.

JACK LONDON claimed to write twenty hours a day. He set his alarm to wake him after four hours' sleep. But, rumor has it, because he often slept through the alarm, he rigged it to drop a weight on his head.

ANTHONY TROLLOPE watched the clock as he wrote, cranking out twelve million words — forty-seven novels, sixty short stories, forty pages per week, two hundred fifty words every quarter hour. This made his friend **GEORGE ELIOT** "quiver with dismay." Trollope, by the way, didn't start writing until he was forty. At age sixty-seven he died of a stroke while laughing at the comic novel he was reading.

LUIGI PIRANDELLO vowed to write one short story for every day of the year. He still had one hundred to go when he died.

A week before she died at ninety-five, **EDITH HAMILTON** said, "You know I haven't felt up to writing, but now I think I am going to be able to finish that book on Plato."

EMILY DICKINSON wrote 1,800 poems, only seven of which were published in her lifetime.

ANTON CHEKHOV wrote more than three hundred short stories.

> A habit is the link between inspiration and self-realization.
>
> ⁓ GAIL SHER ⁓

FRANZ KAFKA completed *The Metamorphosis* in three weeks. An insurance agent by day, he confined his writing to weekends, nights, and vacations.

Historian **SHELBY FOOTE** was reported to write five hundred to six hundred words a day — with a dip pen. It took him twenty years to complete his 1.5 million-word trilogy on the Civil War.

UPTON SINCLAIR wrote eight thousand words every day including Sunday. In an eighteen-month period, while a full-time graduate student at Columbia, he wrote 1,275,000 words.

JACK KEROUAC took tally of his word count in his journal. A November 1944 entry estimated that in the previous five years, since age seventeen, he had logged some 600,000 words — "poems, stories, essays, aphorisms, journals, and nine unfinished novels."

LEO TOLSTOY rewrote *War and Peace* eight times and was still making corrections on the galleys.

> I think we'd all generally acknowledge that it is this particular aspect — drive — that really makes writers, more than even talent, in a way.
>
> ⇝ PETER CAREY ⇜

DONALD BARTHELME wrote every day, seven days a week, and, he said, he threw a lot away. "Sometimes I think I write to throw away; it's a process of distillation."

EUDORA WELTY got up, got her coffee and an "ordinary breakfast," and went to work. At the end of the day, about five or six o'clock, she'd stop, have a bourbon and water, and watch the evening news.

Turkish novelist **ORHAN PAMUK** often rewrites the first line of his novels fifty or one hundred times.

JOSEPH WAMBAUGH said he writes one thousand words a day, minimum, and if an emergency happens and he misses a day, he writes two thousand words the next.

ERICA JONG set herself the task of writing ten pages a day in longhand.

ISABEL ALLENDE writes in a room alone for ten or twelve hours a day, usually Monday through Saturday from 9 AM to 7 PM. During this time, she says, "I don't talk to anybody; I don't answer the telephone. I'm just a medium or an instrument of something that is happening beyond me."

TIM O'BRIEN said he puts in nine-hour days every day — birthdays, Christmas, Halloween — in part because "I love it so much." He also claims to be obsessive.

National Novel Writing Month (NaNoWriMo) writers sign up for 50,000 words during the month of November (1,667 words a day), and some poets pledge to write a poem a day during National Poetry Month (April).

{*See also* Writing Goals, p. 228}

OCTOBER 16 Write about being deserted

OCTOBER 17 If we know of death, we know everything

OCTOBER 18 We left at first light

OCTOBER 19 Our house is full of surprises

OCTOBER 20 Write about a troubled sleep

WRITER'S BLOCK

Writer's block is one of those terms, like *dysfunctional* or *codependent*, that has been used to label so vast a range of symptoms that it's lost any real meaning. Not all interruptions of forward motion are writing blocks, just as not all behavior focused on another is codependent. Sometimes what might appear as a block is merely a pause in the action.

The farmer leaves the ground fallow for a season so it can regenerate itself. So, too, writers need to rest, to refill what has been emptied. Or a writer may be in a stuck place, simply needing a little push to get back to solid ground. Writer's block is a heavy term for such times as these, like using a sledgehammer when the tap of a ball peen would serve. By saying you're suffering from writer's block, you may scare yourself into something that's bigger than it needs to be.

> People have writer's block not because they can't write, but because they despair of writing eloquently.
>
> ⬿ ANNA QUINDLEN ⬿

Some writers don't believe in writer's block. Jamaica Kincaid said writer's block is just another part of writing, and Gordon Lish used the term *writer's search* rather than *writer's block*.

In her book *On Writer's Block*, Victoria Nelson wrote, "Although it can be triggered by any number of internal or external stimuli, the vital function that writer's block performs during the creative process remains constant: *inability to write means that the unconscious self is vetoing the program demanded by the conscious ego.*" In other words, it is not the block itself that is the problem, but the approach the writer is taking to the creative work. Following is a list of potential causes and some solutions for an inability to write.

- **Expectations and perfectionism:** The piece may not be emerging as you intended or as you wanted. It's as foreign as an okapi. And not nearly as perfect.
- **Anxiety:** Fear of failure, fear of success. Fear of finishing, fear of not being able to finish. Fear of any kind. Making art of any kind is fraught with anxiety.
- **Fear of confrontation:** Some writers are as afraid of confrontation in their fiction as they are in their lives; this can cause problems in writing just as it does in real life.

- **Genre confusion in your work:** Maybe the piece you're writing doesn't fit the mold you've chosen. Trying to fit a novel into a short story is like trying to limit a zucchini plant to zero population growth. Reshape the piece or change the mold.

- **Genre confusion in your identity as a writer:** Are you trying to fit yourself into a mold, or conversely, to break out of one? Maybe you're the short story writer who longs to be a novelist, the nonfiction writer who thinks "real" writers write fiction, the children's writer who believes it's time to mature into adult pieces. Rainer Maria Rilke advised, "One may do anything; this alone corresponds to the whole breadth life has. But one must be sure not to take it upon oneself out of opposition, out of spite toward hindering circumstances, or, with others in mind, out of some kind of ambition." In other words, attempt anything, but check your motives.

> Creative blockage is the inability to manage the anxiety that attends the creative process.
>
> ⌒ ERIC MAISEL ⌒

- **A sense of being overwhelmed:** You're only fifty pages into your novel and you know you have at least three hundred to go, plus all those rewrites. We're talking years. The enormity of this is daunting. Remember, writing happens word by word, and novels get written scene by scene.

- **Counterproductive lifestyle and work habits:** Maybe you're trying to write when you're too tired or you're not getting enough rest or exercise. How's your diet? Too much caffeine, not enough fruits and veggies?

- **Times of stress or transition:** Are you in the throes of a challenge such as illness, divorce or separation, job difficulties, or relocation? Any of these can cause a temporary block. Now may not be the time to write.

{*See also* How to Get Unstuck, p. 148}

THE MOST HUMAN ART

TEN REASONS WHY WE'LL ALWAYS NEED A GOOD STORY

BY SCOTT RUSSELL SANDERS

1. We delight in stories because they are a playground for language, an arena for exercising this extraordinary power.

2. Stories create community. They link teller to listeners, and listeners to one another.

3. Stories help us to see through the eyes of other people. Through stories we reach across the rifts not only of gender and age, but also of race and creed, geography and class, even the rifts between species or between enemies.

4. Stories show us the consequences of our actions. To act responsibly, we must be able to foresee where our actions might lead; and stories train our sight.

5. Stories educate our desires. Instead of playing on our selfishness and fear, stories give us images for that which is truly worth seeking, worth having, worth doing.

6. Stories help us dwell in place. Stories of place help us recognize that we belong to the earth, blood and brain and bone, and that we are kin to other creatures.

7. Stories help us dwell in time. History is public, a tale of influences and events that have shaped the present; the mind's time is private, a flow of memory and anticipation that continues, in eddies and rapids, for as long as we are conscious. Narrative orients us in both kinds of time, public and private.

8. Stories help us deal with suffering, loss, and death. Stories reek with our obsession with mortality.

9. Stories teach us how to be human. We are creatures of instinct, but not solely of instinct. More than any other animal, we must *learn* how to behave.

10. Stories acknowledge the wonder and mystery of Creation. [They] give us hope of finding meaning within the great mystery.

{

OCTOBER 21   Write about a suspicion

OCTOBER 22   You're traveling. You're not alone.

OCTOBER 23   What's locked behind glass

OCTOBER 24   A room with no windows

OCTOBER 25   Write about a sleight of hand

}

THE DISCIPLINE OF WRITING

Discipline comes from the Latin for "teaching, learning." Discipline is about being a pupil, being teachable. "The discipline of the writer is to learn to be still and listen to what his subject has to tell him," said Rachel Carson.

Discipline also means self-control. Writers need discipline — to be a student to their writing, to learn about it and from it; and they must have the self-control that will finally get the work done.

"Writing is as much discipline as it is desire," said Christopher Bohjalian. "Don't wait until you're inspired, because if you do, you'll never finish anything."

Discipline means showing up at the page when you said you would. It means staying with a piece to completion, working through the problems as they arise. It means writing when you don't feel like writing or you're not "in the mood." Discipline is turning down invitations that interfere with your writing, and arranging appointments so that they mold around your writing time, not break it up.

> What I believe in as a writer and a teacher, is dedication. And stubbornness. And discipline.
>
> ⌐ BRET ANTHONY JOHNSTON ⌐

When John Keats advised fellow poet Percy Bysshe Shelley to "curb your magnanimity," he wrote, "The thought of such discipline must fall like cold chains upon you, who perhaps never sat with your wings furled for six months together."

Discipline can be hard to come by. Writing isn't easy work. No art is. Staying with it as you slog through problems, as you face the blank page, as, word by word, you expose yourself on paper can take every bit of self-control. A story circulated of one writer who tied the belt of his silk dressing gown to the arms of his chair just to keep himself at his desk.

All this doesn't mean *discipline* is a dirty word, some Ebenezer Scrooge that demands all of you and gives no quarter for fun or lightness or laughter. In fact, the opposite is true. Discipline is a loving act, returning to you the rewards of work completed — how else do you finish a 300-page novel, 120 pages of screenplay, a 3,000-word essay, except with the discipline of writing a page or a line or a word at a time? Discipline also gives you time without burden. Eudora Welty said that when she'd finished her day's work, "I could do anything I wanted."

Being a writer, or any kind of artist, takes commitment and tremendous discipline. The thing is, no one really cares if we do it. Certainly those who love us and who know us urge us on and support us because they know that when we're doing what we are meant to do, we are happier, more complete. They care. But the world doesn't care if we make art. We must care. Charles Dickens wrote, "Whoever is devoted to an Art must be content to deliver himself wholly up to it and find his recompense in it."

> For me, it's more important to keep the discipline of finishing things than to be assured at every moment that it's worth doing.
>
> ⁀ TOBIAS WOLFF ⁀

{*See also* Daily Routine, p. 21; Ten Daily Habits That Make a (Good) Writer, p. 39; Writing Goals, p. 228}

OCTOBER 26	It rained all night
OCTOBER 27	Write about a pilgrimage
OCTOBER 28	He (she) died of _____
OCTOBER 29	You're underwater
OCTOBER 30	Someone's flirting with you
OCTOBER 31	At the matinee

BEYOND PRACTICE

A WALK IN THE WOODS

It is fall, just past the equinox. The light has changed and tones are golden. There is a quieting now, a settling in. This is a good time to take your notebook for a walk in the woods. Go with a friend, if you like. Allow an easy morning or afternoon. Be prepared to slow down.

When you begin, walk for a long time, trying not to think but to simply be. Walk not in order to arrive but just to walk. "It is a great art to saunter," Henry David Thoreau told us. Pause when you will to examine the intricacies of a tree, its branches stretching up and out, the veins in a leaf, the tracks of a creature. No need for conversation. Better to walk in silence, to notice and observe. Listen to the symphony of the place, the play of sound against sound. Let the geometries of light lead you deeper into the woods, and the trail that you follow be the one less traveled.

> There's something about the rhythms of language that correspond to the rhythms of our own bodies.
>
> ⌒ PAUL AUSTER ⌒

"We need the tonic of wildness.... We can never have enough of nature," Thoreau wrote. "I went to the woods because I wished to live deliberately, to front only the essential facts of life, and see if I could not learn what it had to teach, and not, when I came to die, discover that I had not lived."

Returning to the woods, to walk among the wild, refills a part of us we may not even know we have emptied. I have witnessed friends be moved to tears by a feeling of homecoming. I have experienced my own tears. It doesn't seem so strange to embrace a tree, to stand close and lean your body against its solid trunk, surround it with your arms, and press your cheek into its rough bark. Not so strange to wear dwindling flowers in your hair and encircle your wrists with vines. To be on hands and knees, tracking the trail of termites into log, ants into rotting seedpod. To notice the backlit weave of spiderweb and sink into the soft mulch of earth. "You will find something more in woods than in books," wrote St. Bernard of Clairvaux. "Trees and stones will teach you that which you can never learn from masters."

Finally, finally, find a place to sit, remove your notebook from your pack, and open to a blank page. Listen. Breathe in, and pause before you write.

The woods, the wild, the way the light falls and the air smells, prompts for writing surround you. Here are some more, in case you need them.

- Write an October memory
- "A slight sound at evening lifts me up..." (after Henry David Thoreau)
- Surviving twilight
- This is what was left behind
- Write about something out of the past

You're a writer and that's something better than being
a millionaire — because it is something holy.

— HARLAN ELLISON

GUIDELINE 11

READ YOUR WRITING ALOUD

After you've completed your writing session, read what you've written aloud
to yourself or someone else. Reading aloud lets you know how your writer's
mind works. It tells you when you're writing with authenticity and when
you're telling the truth.

Reading aloud after writing practice isn't for feedback or critique of the
work; it's too raw and unfinished for that. Rather, hearing it aloud allows
you to experience the truth of a piece, to discover the depth of emotion it
holds for you. And, because in writing practice you're working more from intuition than planning, you get to find out what you actually put down on
paper. You get to hear your writer's voice.

Reading aloud serves other purposes, too. You hear the repetition in word
usage as well as sentence structure. You pick up clichés and sense obstacles
that might get in the way of the reader. You hear what's working and what
needs work. Allan Gurganus said, "There's a kind of ear music that operates
as an editorial principle on the page even when a reader is not moving his or
her lips." Reading aloud enables you to hear this "ear music," or create it if
it's missing.

To get started on the day's writing, John Barth recommended you read aloud what you've written the day before. "It's to get the rhythm partly, and partly it's a kind of magic: it *feels* like you're writing, though you're not."

When you read aloud, read as if you were standing even though you are sitting down. No mumbling. You honor your words and your writer-self when you read your work aloud.

TIP OF THE MONTH

Keep your exclamation points under control. You're allowed no more than two or three per 100,000 words of prose.

— ELMORE LEONARD

NOVEMBER 1	"This is not my home" (after Elizabeth Bishop)	
NOVEMBER 2	An unmarked box	
NOVEMBER 3	"Every night we save ourselves" (after Jaime Sabines)	
NOVEMBER 4	Write what happened between one moment and the next	
NOVEMBER 5	Walking at night through solitary streets	

TRANSFERRING REAL LIFE TO FICTION

Fiction writers have always used real life experiences as a source for material. In fact, any writer would be hard put to *not* include some of real life in his or her writing, and why shouldn't it be used? Most fictional fires start with real life sparking against imagination.

Whether primarily autobiographical or mostly imagined, all stories contain some of each element. Ann Beattie, who claims she's never written anything directly autobiographical, said, "At the same time I've never written anything that didn't honestly reflect some emotional state." Emotional honesty is the litmus test for successful fiction, and real life is the source for emotions.

Believability is another criterion. So even if "that's the way it really happened," some facts of real life simply won't play in fictional stories. "The difference between truth and fiction is that fiction has to make sense," said Mark Twain. Never mind that some of what we absolutely believe in fiction could never happen in real life. Or could it? Believability is about whether the events of the story or the behavior of a character ring true with the story as a whole.

Rearranging facts, compositing characters, altering time frames and locations — these are some of the ways to transfer the stuff of real life into fiction. "The trick, of course, comes in molding the factual material to the specifications of one's fictional world," said Robin Hemley in *Turning Life into Fiction*. You must be flexible and willing to change the events and facts for the sake of the story. Sometimes what you need is a little distance. That, and a hefty dose of imagination.

> Remember that in the particularity of your own life lies the seedcorn that will feed your imaginative work.
>
> ⟣ ROSE TREMAIN ⟢

"I've always been a writer who has written from someplace reasonably close to experience," said Salman Rushdie, "but it's always used, turned into something, put somewhere else, made something of."

{*See also* Writing about Real People, p. 155; It's All Copy, p. 236; Truth versus Fact, p. 114}

WORDPLAY

Taking your writing seriously doesn't mean giving up the fun of it. Playing with words — squeezing out the sound of them, arranging them on the page in nonsensical visual dollops — is a delightful way to get some fun back into your work. When your writing begins to feel like manual labor under the August sun, lighten up with these playful tools.

- Write the words you love (because of the way they look on the page, the way they sound) helter-skelter on a piece of paper. Play with the look of them. Make big loopy *L*s and round-as-a-baby's-tummy *O*s. Use colored pencils or pens. Or crayons. Don't think about which words to write; let your intuitive choose. In this exercise, the meaning of the words doesn't mean diddly. This wordplay activity is about the visual and aural qualities of the words. Each time you play with words, you'll come up with new loves. You're not fickle; you're expansive.

> As writers we make beautiful objects out of a shared and collective experience of language.
>
> ⮞ BRENDA HILLMAN ⮜

- Choose one of your words from the previous exercise and use it in a sentence. Now make another sentence with another word. Make a whole paragraph using your words. Read them aloud. Resonate with their sound; savor them in your mouth and as they pass through your ears.

- See how many words you can come up with for a color, or a taste, or a sound. Try fifty words for the color orange, do twenty-five on drum, sixteen on sweet. Keep these in your notebook so you can refer to them.

- Create your own thesaurus with these wordplay exercises. Make listings for the color of sky, the shape of clouds, the smell of rain; the contours of chins, noses, eyes; the sounds of laughter, crying, wonder, worry.

- On index cards or construction paper (something thicker than plain printer paper), make a list of words, either by hand or on your computer, leaving enough space to cut them apart. Use nouns and verbs, a few adjectives. Make a word container out of a cool box or jar or basket. Place the cut-apart words in your container and mix them up. Close your eyes and let your fingers find words to start you on a practice session. Select several to start a poem or create an image. Keep adding words to your word container and keep it nearby as you write.

- In the midst of a practice session, dig into your jar of words for a word to use in your next sentence. Don't stop to look for a word, or think about how to use it . . . just go.

- Poet Susan Wooldridge advised us in her book *Poemcrazy* to use manuals or reference books to find words. Mine car repair, home repair, woodworking manuals; look in field guides for birds of the Pacific Coast, Appalachian wildflowers, fly-fishing lures, bats, butterflies. Scour cookbooks, pottery books, sewing and glass-blowing books.

- Describe the way something sounds by using color words; write the way something tastes with mood words; use texture words or emotion words or taste words for the weather.

> The sound of language is where it all begins and what it all comes back to. The basic elements of language are physical: the noise words make and the rhythm of their relationships.
>
> ⁀ URSULA LeGUIN ⁀

- Clip words out of magazines and newspapers to make word collages.

- Open the dictionary to any page and let your eye choose a word to prompt a writing session. Search out unusual words and say them out loud. Take turns with a friend to choose a page number, then find a word on that page to give each other for writing prompts.

- In your portable notebook, list the words you notice in a day — on a walk, in a café, on menus, marquees, signs, bus boards, and billboards. These could be the beginnings of a found poem. List the words that find their way in through your ears as well as your eyes.

- Ernest Hemingway wrote, "There were many words that you could not stand to hear and finally only the names of places had dignity." Write the names of places. Rivers and towns, rocks, plains, mountains, seas. Secret and sacred places of your own making, public places like beaches and baths, neighborhoods and hideouts.

- Make a list of the jobs you've had and the verbs that describe the work you performed: hairdresser (wash, style, trim, cut, color, comb), cook (fry, sauté, chop, braise, roast), waitress, bank teller, lawyer, bartender, mechanic, woodworker, massage therapist. Go beyond paying jobs to work you've done at home: painter (mix, stir, spackle, brush, stroke, roll, tape), gardener (dig, spade, plant, transplant, hoe, weed), chauffeur, cook, builder, bricklayer, nurse, seamstress, interior designer.

A number of years ago, the *Oxford English Dictionary* listed about half a million words, plus another half million technical and scientific terms. These days, unabridged English dictionaries contain 650,000 to 750,000 words. In contrast, German has a vocabulary of about 185,000, and French, fewer than 100,000. But, as they say, it's not about quantity; it's about quality. The right word at the right time.

THE WRITING LIFE

WHERE THEY GOT THEIR IDEAS

The idea for *Hay Fever* came to **NOËL COWARD** as he walked in a garden. He wrote it in three days.

KATHERINE ANNE PORTER said her writing began with an idea forming like a dark cloud. *Ship of Fools* began as notes in her journal and took thirty years to complete.

MICHAEL ONDAATJE's *The English Patient* drew on the life of Count László Almásy. "I used the first part of his life then moved on into fiction."

> Doubt and uncertainty are not only a part of, but are fundamental to, the writing process. Not knowing is crucial to the making of a novel. It sets wonder in motion.
>
> ⮑ JOHN DUFRESNE ⮐

In **JOHN BARTH**'s book *The Floating Opera*, the floating showboat came from a photograph of an actual showboat he remembered from his childhood. It happened to be named *Captain Adams' Original Unparalleled Floating Opera*.

RAYMOND CARVER's story "Why Don't You Dance?" came from visiting writer friends in Missoula, Montana, in the mid-1970s. Someone told a story about a barmaid named Linda who got drunk with her boyfriend one night and decided to move all her bedroom furnishings into the backyard. "They did it, too, right down to the carpet and the bedroom lamp, the bed, the nightstand, everything."

ERICA JONG, who promised herself that she would write a Fieldingesque novel set in that period (eighteenth-century England), said the idea for her book *Fanny: Being the True History of the Adventures of Fanny Hackabout-Jones* really started with the simple question, What if Tom Jones had been a woman?

GERALDINE BROOKS was walking in the hills near Derbyshire, England, when she got the idea for *Year of Wonders*, but it wasn't until she lived in a small village in the Blue Ridge foothills of Virginia that she was able to imagine the lives of 250 souls who quarantined themselves during the plague.

LEO TOLSTOY's character Anna Karenina was reportedly inspired by Maria Hartung, eldest daughter of Alexander Pushkin. The novel *Anna Karenina* was first serialized in a Russian periodical.

NOVEMBER 11   The blue of pool water

NOVEMBER 12   Relics of a distant past

NOVEMBER 13   Write about waking up

NOVEMBER 14   Three days of hard freeze

NOVEMBER 15   "An unspoken hunger" (after Terry Tempest Williams)

HOW TO TELL WHEN YOUR ENGLISH TEACHER IS PRESENT

When imaginary Rules of Composition and Grammar accompanied by righteous comments and precise little check marks surface between the lines on your page as if written in invisible red ink, you can almost hear your old English teacher tsking in your ear and smell her chicken-soup breath. (This isn't the Glinda the Good Witch teacher who wrote "Great Imagination" in her generous handwriting on your homework and laughed out loud at your stories. Or my eleventh grade English teacher, Mrs. Gatos, who introduced me to e. e. cummings and taught me it was okay to break the rules. No, this is the Wicked Witch of the West teacher who drilled you in coordinate conjunctions and present progressive tense, who would not abide dangling participles, especially if they were past perfect.)

> Don't worry about your personal writing style....Just learn to write well, and your style will emerge.
>
> ☞ GARY PROVOST ☜

How do you know when your English teacher is present? Here's what to look for and how to get around it.

- You worry over the structure of a sentence, rather than what it conveys.

    Say what you want to say, then clean it up later. Don't even worry if you're writing complete, proper sentences, at least not in practice.
- You're concerned about whether you've included all the elements of composition — the introductory paragraph with your thesis and how you're going to prove it, supporting paragraphs with specific examples, and a concluding statement that restates your thesis.

    Don't get caught up in beginnings, middles, and endings. Just write. Let the piece stand on its own. "There is nothing to prove and everything to imagine," said Eugène Ionesco. You can rearrange, add to, and take from during rewrites.

- You get held ransom by semicolons, and grammar flummoxes you.

  Don't worry about grammar or punctuation. Just write.

- All this talk about active vs. passive voice paralyzes you into no voice at all. Same with tenses — present, past, past perfect — they've got you all tensed up.

  It's not unusual for pieces composed during the intensity of writing practice to be inconsistent in style and for time to travel from past to present and back again. Even names get changed and pronouns switch gender from one paragraph to the next. With practice, writers can train themselves to write in the active rather than the passive voice. Rewriting teaches. And with each piece you write and rewrite, you get to make any number of choices, including whether to use past or present tense. Listen closely as you reread your piece aloud; sometimes the tense that best suits the piece will appear.

> You write to communicate to the hearts and minds of others what's burning inside you. And you edit to let the fire show through the smoke.
>
> ⌒ ARTHUR PLOTNIK ⌒

- You're afraid to simply follow your pen. What if you clutter your paragraph with material that strays from your main point?

  Because it works in symbols and imagery, the intuitive mind connects the dots in ways that our thinking mind might never see. Let go and trust your pen. Sometimes the debris that is left in the wake of your wild mind turns out to be your main point.

- What you're writing doesn't seem to fit into any form you studied in school. When someone asks, "What are you writing?" you don't know how to answer.

  Labeling your work can stifle it, especially in its early stages. Let form come organically out of the work itself. When someone asks what you're writing and you don't know, it's okay to answer, "I don't know. It hasn't told me yet."

- The freewheeling idea of going outside the lines, using *all* the page with handwriting that looks as if it has a life of its own, is held in check by the nagging reminder "Neatness counts."

When you hold back your handwriting, you also hold back ideas. Just for the heck of it, open to a clean, unmarred page in your notebook and let 'er rip. Disregard the margins, the lines, even the need to write linearly. Fill the page with messy, expressive, out-of-control handwriting. With chaos for a mother and imagination for a father, creativity wasn't raised on neat and tidy.

{*See also* Guideline 5: Don't Worry about the Rules, p. 83}

DISCOVER WHAT YOU WANT TO WRITE ABOUT

When I ask students in my writing classes what they want to write about, I often get big, broad answers like, "I want to write about my life in the military" or "I want to write about my crazy family." Or, they answer with widespreading generalities like "the relationship of mothers and daughters" or "the sixties."

Whoever said "It's better to write about God's hat than God," was suggesting that rather than tackling expansive subjects that have no beginning, middle, or end, it's better to narrow your subject down to some specifics. Specific incidents, times, relationships. When my student Steve wrote about the time his character lost the company's bulldog mascot, he was writing about life in the military. Jodi, another student, wrote about the Thanksgiving dinner when Uncle Hendrick wore Aunt Lilly's chemise under his blue-striped shirt and Aunt Lilly choked on the giblets. This created immediate and specific examples of a crazy family.

Incident by incident, example by example, these specifics will gather a momentum of their own, and the story that wants to be written will come organically out of the collected pieces, which you'll craft into a beginning, middle, and end. You may not use every one of the pieces, but all of them will be useful in helping you find the story. In writing, as in love, nothing is wasted.

> When you're writing, don't ask what happens next, ask what happened next and then see it and write down what did.
>
> ⌁ JOHN DUFRESNE ⌁

To find out what you want to write about, try this: On a clean sheet of paper, begin a sentence with "I want to write about..." Before your brain has a chance to kick in, grab a corner of the first image that comes to you and pin it down in a few sentences. Include specifics of time, place, people, and some sensory details. As soon as you have completed your paragraph (no more than four or five sentences), begin the next "I want to write about..." and once again, nab the image and begin writing it. Repeat this exercise until you've filled your page. Don't stop to think between paragraphs, and avoid generalities.

If none of your images relate in any way to what you thought you wanted to write about, you may consider this a message from your intuitive self to your thinking self. Maybe you thought writing about the history of women sounded more important than writing about the relationship between your mother and her sisters. But what is the history of women except an eternity of specific relationships?

To keep your "I want to write abouts" within a particular subject and to help focus your paragraphs, write a headline across the top of your page — such as *Family Stories* — and limit your listings to that subject area. Once again, don't stop to think of what you want to write; simply begin the paragraph with "I want to write about . . ." The directive of the headline and your intention will help focus your writing. Note: if images that don't relate to your subject continue to appear, pay attention and be willing to listen to your inner writer.

I'm a great believer in lists. Lists are a kind of mental shorthand, a fast way to get control of things. Lists can also help you find out what you want to write about. In her book *Journal to the Self*, psychotherapist and journal-writing teacher Kathleen Adams taught me the value of making lists of one hundred items.

> The discipline of the writer is to learn to be still and listen to what his subject has to tell him.
>
> ⁓ RACHEL CARSON ⁓

Briefly, here's how to do it: Number your page from 1 to 100, then, as quickly as you can and without thinking (just like in writing practice), make a list of one hundred things you want to write about. Use single words or short phrases only, no details. Don't worry about repetition; repeated entries emphasize a topic's importance to you. Just get it down. Try making lists of one hundred memories, one hundred intriguing situations, one hundred questions I want answers to, and one hundred mysteries.

A surefire way to discover what you want to write is by uncovering what you have already written about. Within your notebook is a Hansel and Gretel trail of images, phrases, and words that appear and reappear. When you reread your notebooks, follow these bread crumbs through the forest of your writing. They will lead you home.

{*See also* Images That Haunt You, p. 153; Rereading Your Practice Pages, p. 185; Create Your Own Writing Topics, p. 231}

TELL YOUR SECRETS

Revealing secrets is one of the dangers of being a writer. By laying yourself open to the page or whoever reads it you chance exposure every time you write. Even baring yourself to yourself can be frightening. "Being a poet is a damned dangerous business," said Carl Sandburg. Prose is no less dangerous. But if you don't write your secrets, if you tiptoe nervously around whatever you've got concealed, you risk creating vague and untrustworthy writing. Also, holding back some things means being guarded about other things. The sentinel at your palace door is going to ask, "Who goes there?" of every thought that might be cloaked in danger or intrigue. Woe be to the writer whose palace guard is paranoid and every thought suspect.

> Nothing that happens to a writer — however happy, however tragic — is ever wasted.
>
> ⁓ P. D. JAMES ⁓

Divulging secrets, whether to yourself in your notebook, to your writing group, or to an even bigger audience, might be an experience you want to work up to. Here are some suggestions.

- Write a secret on a blank page, then tear it up or burn it. The act of getting it out and on paper takes much of the power out of confidences. Write as many pages as you have secrets. Build a bonfire if you need to. (You don't have to do this all in one sitting; take as many sessions as you need. Do it each time you remember another secret.)

- In a writing group, have each member anonymously write a secret on a slip of paper. Fold them up, drop them in a basket, and invite each person to draw one and use it as a writing prompt. If someone gets her own secret, it could be the Muse saying now's the time to write about it. If that doesn't feel right, have everyone return the secrets to the basket and redraw.

- Give your confidences to a fictional character (make her smart and beautiful and very rich) and let her tell them.

- Ease into "that which you can never tell" like a stripteaser doing his or her act, revealing just a little at a time, first a wrist, then a shoulder. Stop when you feel you've gone far enough.

{*See also* Take Risks, p. 132; How to Tell When the Censor Is Present, p. 175; Avoiding the Truth, p. 98}

GIFTS OF THE NIGHT: HOW TO USE YOUR DREAMS

Images that appear in the night can find their way into your writing. Dreams can solve problems and answer questions, invite the opening of a door, the looking out of a window or into a room. Characters appear with messages and meanings. Your dream life can influence your writing life, and your creative work can alter your dreams. And sometimes not even you can say what it all means. How do you use your dreams in your writing life?

- Keep a dream notebook beside your bed to write down dreams in the morning or when they awaken you in the night. Write them when you first wake up. You may think you will remember them later, but chances are you won't. Even the most powerful dreams can be as elusive as gossamer in the light of day. Try to capture the details and sketch the images. Then make use of the surreal, nonsensical, imaginative, and surprising imagery of the dreams in your writing.

> Writing fiction for me is like remembering what never happened.
>
> ⮞ SIRI HUSTVEDT ⮜

- Many believe you can ask for a dream. If you're at a stuck place or need a solution to a problem in your writing, ask the dream maker to bring you answers in the night. Invite your characters in, too.
- Give your dreams to your characters. If you have a recurring dream of daylilies breaking through the snow, loons flying overhead, or water seeping into your house, let your characters use the dream. Consider what the dreams might mean to the characters and how they might interpret them.
- Use a dream as a starting place for a practice session. Begin with "I dreamed..." and complete the exercise as you would the "I remember..." exercise. You may be surprised at the dreams you recall using this technique.

{*See also* The Writing Life: Writers on Dreaming, p. 112}

BREATHE

Breathing is the link between our body and our mind. Sometimes we are so out of our bodies, we forget to breathe. Conscious breathing and then allowing our breath to set the rhythm of our writing will connect us.

If the piece you're writing carries great emotion, or if you are frightened by what you're writing, you may hold your breath. When this happens, your body becomes tense, the emotion builds, and fear grows until the tension is so great the only way to relieve it is to stop writing. So you put the pen down, close your notebook, and get up from your desk. The tension is relieved, but the piece you were writing, with its intensity and raw honesty, is lost, maybe gone forever.

> To pay attention, this is our endless and proper work.
>
> ◠ MARY OLIVER ◠

Try this: As you are writing and you sense the tension building, breathe into the feeling and continue writing. This can cause emotions to release, and you may begin crying. If this happens, just keep breathing and keep your pen moving. Or you may experience anger that you were trying to hold back by holding your breath. Breathe into the feeling and write the anger; write as big and bold as you need, pressing the pen into the page even to the point of tearing it. Soon you'll find that you've passed through to the other side of the emotion, and calmness has returned; breathing has allowed you to experience the feeling, and writing has enabled you to express it.

At other times, it may not be the heightened emotions that cause you to stop breathing but the incredible energy of the piece you are writing. You get pulled into its intensity and not only forget to breathe but grip your pen so tightly you experience muscle cramps. Again, breathe into the writing and relax your hold on your pen but don't stop writing. Breathing will help you keep your balance as you ride the crest of the wave until, finally, its energy dissipates and you roll safely to shore.

"Breathing, we bring our body and mind back together and become whole again," said Thich Nhat Hanh. Breathing carries oxygen to the brain, grounds us physically, and provides a rhythm for our work.

Writing is a holistic act. To be completely present, use your mind, your body, and your soul. Breathing is the cord that binds all three together.

WHEN CAN I QUIT MY DAY JOB AND BE A FULL-TIME WRITER?

Expecting to earn a living as a writer may be expecting too much. Especially for beginners. The fact is, only a small percentage of all writers in the United States earn enough money from their writing to support themselves. Many writers who've sold three, four, or five books still have to work at other jobs. And the payment for short stories is often in contributor's copies of the publication. "I thought that I would always have to have a day job and write in the evening," said Margaret Atwood.

The hard reality is, as a writer, you may be facing years of fitting your writing into a schedule that includes working a full- or part-time job. Add to that a family, friends, and other responsibilities, and the romantic version of the writer's life that includes big advances, acres of time, interviews, book signings, and a spacious, book-lined study — that version of the writer's life wavers and disappears like a mirage on a long and lonesome blacktop highway.

> The key to a successful writing career is to be born brilliant, with flawless work habits, little need for sleep, and wealthy grandparents who own prestigious magazines and publishing houses.
>
> ⌒ DINTY W. MOORE ⌒

If you've determined you want writing to have preeminence in your life, some reconstruction may be in order. You may have to change jobs to make more time for writing, even though it might mean less income; to simplify; to move to a smaller, less expensive place; to make choices between vacations and writing, entertainment and writing, sometimes friends and family and writing, even sleep and writing. Will it be worth it? "People say poets can't make a living. I tell them to lower their expectations to match their income," said Nikki Giovanni.

If you expect to write and get rich, you will probably be disappointed. Rich writers are as rare as ostriches in Alaska. On the other hand, if you write because this is how you are made and, like Raymond Carver who took refuge in the car with a pad on his knee or novelist Sara Lewis who shut herself in the laundry room at 4:30 in the morning, you write because you can't *not* write, it is simply what you do, and whether or not it's worth it is a moot point — if you're this kind of writer, there is no other way.

But for another kind of writer, the one who is not driven by a passion that gives no sway, and who accepts the reality that he may never be self-supporting through his writing efforts, and who will always have to make choices between writing and something else, will it be worth it?

Rainer Maria Rilke wrote, "Ask yourself in the quietest hour of your night: must I write? Dig down into yourself for the deep answer. And if this should be in the affirmative, if you may meet this solemn question with a strong and simple, I must, then build your life according to this necessity."

> Keep a low overhead. You're not going to make a lot of money.
>
> ⌐ GRACE PALEY ⌐

BEYOND PRACTICE

A FIELD TRIP TO THE LIBRARY

What better ingredient for your writing than the sacrosanct dust of a library. It's a virtual literary surround-sound, a place of order and generosity within an aromatic maze that is more than wood and paper and ink and glue and dust and time gone by. "My library was dukedom large enough," Prospero avowed in *The Tempest*.

For this Beyond Practice session, take your notebook on a field trip to your local library. (Remember the first time you entered a library?) Meander the stacks and gather books that call out to you. Fiction, poetry, art and photography, nonfiction, biographies, essays, books on time and place and history, compendiums, compilations, anthologies, collections. Children's books, cookbooks, science and technology books. Any book and every book that whispers, *Read me, read me*. Carry your armload of treasures to some quiet table and build a fort of books around you. Take your time and open one book at random; let the Muse choose the page. Savor the words as you read them, gaze into images, allow colors and shapes to amaze you. Let them inspire you to write.

Follow images that lead you into writing, or use phrases, sentences, or lines of poetry as prompts. Read, then write, then read again; allow a rhythm to arise from the taking in and giving out. Impression and expression. Impose a specific amount of time for each or let the natural flow that emerges be your guide. Remind yourself that there is no hurry. Just because you've selected fourteen books doesn't mean you have to look inside every one or use something from each for a writing prompt. Trust that the right book is the one in your hands, find what it has to tell you, then move to the next. If you don't get to all the books you've chosen, know that there will be another time, another library day, another Beyond Practice session. And if your library card is current, you can always check out an armload of books to take home.

> What do I do? There are twenty-six letters in the alphabet. I jumble them around.
>
> ⌒ MORDECAI RICHLER ⌒

The best part: so long as people continue actively, vocally, and passion-ately using, supporting, and promoting our public libraries, the libraries will be there with their amazing abundance of books and media available for all of us.

Suggested prompts, though you'll hardly need them:

- Write about bodies of water
- Write about something that belongs to someone else
- This is what woke me up
- It was before ...
- It was postmarked Pocatello

{ DECEMBER }

Work is not an expression of the desire for praise, or recognition, or prizes,
but the deepest manifestation of your gratitude for the gift of life.

— STANLEY KUNITZ

GUIDELINE 12

DATE YOUR PAGE AND
WRITE THE TOPIC AT THE TOP

Dating your page helps keep you grounded in the present while your writing soars into distant galaxies and travels through time. Noting the date will also give an order to your entries and can be used for gathering information: When was the first time Julio, that slippery character with topaz eyes and dangerous hands, appeared? When did I start writing the loaf of bread story? Is there some kind of synchronicity between my literary glimpses of the moon and the actual moon cycles? What is the rhythm of my writing? Are there specific days when I write with ease and passion and other times when it's like swimming upriver after spring thaw? All these questions and more, dates on your page will readily answer. You'll also be able to track how often you keep your daily writing practice date, as with gold stars on a calendar (which isn't a bad idea either).

By writing the topic at the top of the page you'll be able to reference pieces you might want to use in something else. You can also see how your mind works, the intricate weave of associations and connections. Plus, in review, you may be able to tell which types of prompts are most evocative for you, and which are least. Some writers work best from prompts that are solid and concrete — "Write about a used car you owned" or "You hear church bells in the distance"; others respond better to abstract or vague phrases or images — "Under the surface of ordinary things" or "Aftershocks of the full moon." This is good to know as you create your own topics or look to those ideas that will stretch you.

TIP OF THE MONTH

Never want to say anything so strongly that you give up the option of finding something better.

— RICHARD HUGO

DECEMBER	1	Write about a silver ring
DECEMBER	2	It was her mother's recipe
DECEMBER	3	What washed up on the shore
DECEMBER	4	The map of a daydream
DECEMBER	5	Your earliest memory

HOW TO START
A WRITING PRACTICE GROUP

Writing in a group is an evocative experience for many writers. Some say they write better, take more risks, have more fun, and actually write more than when they write alone. And, almost to a person, they say they learn about writing from the group experience even if there's no actual feedback or critique in the sessions.

Groups can offer support, structure, and variety to the writing practice experience. And there are those who believe that the Muse likes to work crowds.

Meet in cafés, bookstores, or private homes, or in rooms in community centers, libraries, or schools; all you need is a place where you can stay a while, where you won't be distracted during the writing time, and where you can read aloud after you've completed the writing.

To start a writing practice group, you can begin with just one other person. Set up a time and a place, bring notebooks and prompts (or make them up when you get together), and go to it. Take turns offering prompts and keeping time.

To attract more participants, put notices on bulletin boards in cafés or on your community's Craigslist or Meetup. Use Facebook or the latest social media outlet. (Note: if you open the group to the general public, you'll probably want to meet in a public place.) Larger groups mean either longer meeting times or short writing periods so that everyone can have an opportunity to read. Let the group determine how long the sessions should be and how frequently to meet. Use the guidelines on pages 8–9; read them at the opening of each session as a way of beginning and centering.

Happy writing.

{*See also* Find Your Tribe: Why Hang Out with Other Writers, p. 173; Find Support for Your Writing Life, p. 234}

HOW WRITING HEALS

When you write about something that gives rise to pain from the deep place of memory and body where it resides, you literally feel the emotions that surround it. Tears often accompany bringing these feelings to the page. By writing it, you acknowledge the pain and its cause. Acknowledgment is the first step in recovery. When you read your work aloud you give voice to your feelings. These are some of the ways writing heals.

It is an act of courage to complete such writing. Edging toward the pain may feel like nearing the perimeter of a great black hole. This is how it felt when I tried to write about my husband's death. For years I was able to write only fragments, the feathery wing of memory, a muted image. Finally, after a decade, I sketched the skeleton of a story, thin and pale as his body during those final months. As time went on, I returned to the story again and again, each time healing a bit more from the loss. Another decade later, twenty years after his death, the finished piece found its way into a publication.

Amy Tan said, "In the telling of stories something happens, your whole perception and memory of things begins to change and you can let go of what you have just told — you give it away." In letting go, we heal.

> The seeker, however, must seek — and this is the core of his difficulty. He cannot know what he is looking for until he finds it.
>
> ⌒ WILLIAM SEGAL ⌒

Think of how we tell stories when catastrophe strikes. Or when marriages go asunder or relationships end, after injuries or accidents or violence we experience or witness. Again and again we relate the tale. We're on the phone or writing letters or emailing. We stand on street corners, stop mid-aisle in grocery stores; we meet in restaurants, cafés, and bars and say to one another, "This is what happened." It is the nature of humans to recount events, to give way to feelings.

Writing them down helps us accept our experiences and emotions as real — after all, there they are, in black and white. Acceptance is another step in recovery.

More than just a way to express our feelings, writing lets us feel them; it leads us into the deep places of our heart and shines a light so we can bring these stories from inside to outside. This movement creates some space, perhaps just enough to feel our heart beat or take a breath, but enough to let us know we are still alive.

When we hear or read others' stories, we bear witness to their experience, which is healing for them and for us. Through our written and spoken voices we connect in ways that reassure us we are not alone. Realizing that others have the same hungers and longings as we do, that their fears, bewilderment, and pain are the same as ours, allows us to experience our commonality. Only then can we feel compassion. Love follows compassion's footprints and, surely, the healing of great wounds cannot be far beyond this.

In his book *Poetic Medicine: The Healing Art of Poem-Making*, poetry therapist John Fox writes, "Poetry is a natural medicine; it is like a homeopathic tincture derived from the stuff of life itself — *your experience....* Poetry provides guidance, revealing what you did not know you knew before you wrote or read the poem." The same can be said of other types of writing you may do: journaling, freewriting, stream of consciousness — the kinds of writing that emerge when you become unself-conscious and write from that deeper place, the heart place.

Stories that ache to be told are your psyche's way of longing to be healed. Painful though it may be, listen to these urges, take courage, and write them.

{*See also* Being Vulnerable on the Page, p. 123; When Your Writing Embarrasses You, p. 177}

DECEMBER 6	"The first birds are waking into song" (after Roy Scheele)	
DECEMBER 7	Four miles out of town, the highway _____	
DECEMBER 8	This is her (his) fantasy	
DECEMBER 9	7 or 8 things you know about her (after Michael Ondaatje)	
DECEMBER 10	After the last guest left	

DANCE WITH YOUR SHADOWS

As we write, we stumble into hidden recesses of ourselves, those places under the eaves where shadows sway in half-light and croon our names. A seductive tango, raucous rock and roll, a ballet of treachery, writing plays the tune and the writer dances. We may insist that we don't know the steps, but we do, we do.

Our shadow self is that part of us we find unacceptable. This is what psychoanalyst C. G. Jung told us. Somewhere before our second decade we shut her down or put him away, denied and repressed that part of ourselves. The part that grew up to be a tango dancer who wears slinky black dresses and a rose in her hair, so unlike our cotton skirts and Birkenstocks. Or that rock and roller who jumps and shouts and parties all night long when the "real" us is all business suits and Bach.

> Everyone has talent. What is rare is the courage to follow that talent to the dark place where it leads.
>
> ⌒ ERICA JONG ⌒

But shadows don't go away; they follow behind us, matching our every step with their own. Turn quickly and they disappear. Or they spread before us, lurching large and misshapen on the pavement beneath our feet. They come out and dance by the light of the moon.

There's more, too. Where do we find these characters who are capable of stealing babies and trashing hotel rooms, who lie and cheat and set cars on fire? Imagination, yes, and perhaps shadowy urges best left to fiction.

Susan Wooldridge wrote, "To become more fully who we are, it's a good idea to invite our shadow to speak now and then." Give him a few hours and listen to what he can tell you. You'll learn your own secrets and get a different perspective. ("Oh, so that's what it feels like to shoplift." "Peek in someone's window? Why not?")

Use a writing practice session to play "What if . . . ?" What if you gave in to the temptation to look in someone's window? Or what if you actually did stuff that bracelet or those sunglasses or that little crystal bowl into your bag? Use sensory details and concrete images to enter the scene; stay with your body for physical sensations. Stay away from judgments and instead, be the observer.

Make a list of "things I would never do," then choose one from your list and give it to a fictional character to carry out. Maybe you'd never lie to the IRS, but Tiffany sure would. Get inside Tiffany's character and lay a nose-stretcher on Ms. Finkbinder of the IRS.

Go ahead, dance with your shadow. Welcome her with a cup of tea and a sweet cake, if that's what pleases her, or a beer and a smoke — whatever potion or poison will lure her to your table. Roll back the rug, clear away the furniture, and follow your shadow's lead. Then head for your notebook and get it all down while your body still moves to the rhythm she set.

DECEMBER 11   I couldn't see anything but the road in front of me

DECEMBER 12   "Do not fall in love"

DECEMBER 13   At the hour of your birth

DECEMBER 14   The table in the corner

DECEMBER 15   Write about moon shadows

WRITING GOALS

Setting goals is a way to accomplish specific projects and create a discipline for your writing. Some writers use a word count, others a page count, still others, a set amount of time to write every day. Remember Upton Sinclair's ambitious eight thousand words a day? Carolyn See's advice in *Making a Literary Life*, to write "a thousand words a day"? And in *The Artist's Way* Julia Cameron suggests writing "morning pages" (three pages first thing every morning). Page a day; one true sentence; two hours; half hour, five days a week. Everyone, including me, will try to tell you what to do if you want to be a writer. Ultimately, each of us must find our own way.

Work with different goals to find the method that serves you best. Above all, be realistic. If you set your goals too high and can't accomplish them, you may find yourself so discouraged that you give up doing any work at all. Disaster! On the other hand, if you're not stretching, you're not growing as a writer. And open ends have a way of never closing.

Let's say over a period of a few weeks of regular writing practice, you discover that during a fifteen-minute session, you write about 400 words. You could set a goal of 500 words a day, and push yourself another few minutes, with a goal of 2,500 words of raw, first-draft writing each week (writing five days a week). Or make a goal to practice six days a week, or every day. Or stretch your writing time to an hour.

My friend Greg set a goal of working from 9 AM to 2 PM five days a week. Notice I said *working*, not *writing*. During that five hours he may write first-draft material in his notebook, edit what he has written on previous days, rewrite stories he's presented in his read-and-critique group, or study the craft through reading books and journals about writing. He also has his favorite double mocha (no whip, nonfat) and spends some time observing.

> It doesn't make any difference if you are good or bad today. The assessment of the product is something that happens after you've done it.
>
> ⮌ WILLIAM STAFFORD ⮌

Another way of setting goals is to participate in a read-and-critique group that has a fixed number of pages you can submit per session. Maybe eight or ten manuscript pages (double-spaced, wide margins, about 250 words per page) each time. This quota could be your goal. Bear in mind, manuscript pages are not the raw stuff of writing practice. This is work you have rewritten and shaped — material from your notebook distilled and revised into something more polished.

Some writers I know participate in National Novel Writing Month (NaNoWriMo) wherein they commit to writing a 50,000-word novel during the month of November. That's about 1,667 words a day, every day, including Thanksgiving. And while they wouldn't think of keeping that kind of pace every month, the work they do in November gives them a raw piece to work on for the next year (or five).

> The trouble with doing nothing is you never know when you're finished.
>
> ⌒ ANONYMOUS ⌒

Your goals may change as the work changes. You may start a project by writing two hours a day and as the piece takes shape, change the goal to completing a chapter in a week or a revision in a month.

Once you know your speed and tempo, you can set other goals: four short stories completed and submitted this year, first draft of a novel by December, six finished poems this spring. Goal setting is another expression of your commitment to your writing.

{*See also* The Writing Life: Quotas and Other Facts and Figures, p. 189; Daily Routine, p. 21; The Discipline of Writing, p. 195}

DECEMBER 16   Write what is meant to be remembered
DECEMBER 17   "He was the kind of man who…"
DECEMBER 18   He (she) ordered the usual
DECEMBER 19   A one-way ticket
DECEMBER 20   "On my birthday…"

THE WRITING LIFE

WRITERS ON WHY THEY WRITE

GEORGE SAUNDERS said, "I see writing as a part of an ongoing attempt to really, viscerally, believe that everything matters, suffering is real, and death is imminent."

ISABEL ALLENDE sees writing as an act of hope, a communion with our fellow man.

UMBERTO ECO said he is continuously trying to find the meaning of things under the text.

JOHN KEATS wrote for the "mere yearning and fondness" he had for the beautiful. To him, it mattered not if "my night's labors should be burnt every morning and no eye shine upon them."

When asked by a student why she wrote, **EUDORA WELTY** said, "because I'm good at it."

MARY GAITSKILL called stories the "right, unseen underlayer of the most ordinary moments." She said she got great satisfaction from plunging her hands into that underlayer.

> Writing, for me, is an act of faith, a hope that I will discover what I mean by "truth."
>
> ⌒ AMY TAN ⌒

MICHAEL ONDAATJE believes writing links up one's own life with the history of our time.

RICHARD FORD likes the notion that literature is a gift from the writer to the reader.

WILL CARLETON said his purpose in writing is "to touch and draw out that vein of poetry and feeling which exists somewhere in every human nature."

In her stunning essay, "Why I Write," **TERRY TEMPEST WILLIAMS** concludes, "I write as though I am whispering in the ear of the one I love."

In your next practice session write your own response to "Why I write."

CREATE YOUR OWN WRITING TOPICS

It's not that some people don't know what they want to write about — in fact, there is so much they care about, they can become paralyzed by the infinite choice of subjects. Everything is right and nothing is right.

Here are some ideas to help you create your own practice topics.

- Write the words "I remember..." at the top of a blank page. Then, without hesitation, write the next words that come to you. Be specific. Write the details of what you remember, not just the idea of it. As soon as you've completed a few sentences of the image, and before you stop to think of the next, drop down a few lines, leaving a white space to create an opening for a new memory. Start a new paragraph with the words "I remember..." and write the next snapshot that comes. Do it again and again until you've filled a page. Here's an example.

> A writer's lifelong battle...is the battle to sustain the imagination, to discover the tricks of habit that allow invention to proceed in the face of conformity.
>
> ⌒ ETHAN CANIN ⌒

I remember walking that path beside the Adriatic in Brela when it was still Yugoslavia, the gray rocks as big as moving trucks and the piney deep green scent of the trees. I remember being homesick.

I remember drinking cherry Cokes with single, long-stemmed maraschino cherries. The marble-topped back booth at Kruger's Drug Store where Betty Barnes and Sharon Mallory and I giggled and blushed and told boy stories.

I remember driving the road that climbs the mountains behind Santa Barbara the day before Christmas. The morning was crisp as toast with a sky that held blue like it was the one true thing. All around me

the hills yawned and stretched, and above, a hawk landed on a tele-
phone line and eyed me as I cruised by.

Each of these *I remember*s becomes a door into a writing session.

- Stash notepads and pens in all your reading locations (I've got them beside my bed, in a red velvet box on my dining table, tucked in the cushions of the couch, on my desk, in the car). When you come upon a phrase or image that strikes you, write it down. Do this with everything you read — novels, short stories, nonfiction, poetry, newspapers, magazines, and cereal boxes. Once taken out of context, the phrases and images assume a random quality entirely separate from their source. Store these slips of paper in a file folder or envelope that you can dip into on your way to a practice session.

> I keep my mind open all day long, like a net, so I can catch things that will fit nicely into [the book I'm writing].
>
> ⌒ DAVID EBERSHOFF ⌒

- Go within the belly of your own writing for topics. Here you'll find images and phrases of your own making that you can use outside of their original context, just as you can those of other writers.

- As others read aloud from their writing, make notes of phrases that resonate with you. You may want to let your writing friends know you are using their material as a prompt. Not all writers take kindly to such borrowing, while others consider it a compliment.

- Use song lyrics as writing prompts. Try to stay away from the familiar, which would be akin to using a cliché for a prompt, and go toward the lesser known.

- Every day for a month, create a first sentence in your writer's notebook. Don't worry about how or when it might get used or the identity of some character whose name appears in one (or more) of the sentences. After you have a month's worth of these starters, cut them into strips, fold them up, and put them in an envelope. Wait a while until you've all but forgotten what you've written before you begin pulling these for writing topics. Spontaneity is always a good ingredient for a practice session.

On the bookshelf in my writing space is a tiny red satin box filled with words to use as writing prompts. A pale woven straw box with a lid contains strips of sentence stems, folded and waiting; a rotund basket spills over with my postcard collection. Envelopes stuffed with writing topics are secreted between books; a shallow wooden bowl holds clippings from a book of poems. On the shelf next to a round-faced clock leans a tall red loose-leaf notebook, its pages lined with topics from past practice sessions, to be used again or not. Create your own library of writing practice prompts. You'll never be at a loss of what to write about.

{*See also* Discover What You Want to Write About, p. 210; Rereading Your Practice Pages, p. 185}

DECEMBER 21   Write about a shortcut
DECEMBER 22   Write about one precious thing lost
DECEMBER 23   The sound of a thousand secrets
DECEMBER 24   In the garden after dark
DECEMBER 25   Hidden in a corner

FIND SUPPORT FOR YOUR WRITING LIFE

Whether it's in the DNA or a dowry that's doled out by the gods — "you be a painter, you a musician, you a chef, you a teacher, you a writer" — or perhaps something more random or even more holy, the gift of writing isn't given to everyone. Choosing a writing life means honoring that gift. It sets you a little or a lot outside the norm and makes you a part of a world others might find different, odd, foreign. Because the writing life does go outside the lines, family, coworkers and bosses, and certain friends may not be the best source of support for writers. Yet support is what all artists need. Here's a list of people and places to find encouragement, assistance, and friends along the way, and why writers need this.

> The only thing you should have to do is find work you love to do.
>
> ⌒ GRACE PALEY ⌒

- **Writing friends:** Especially one or maybe two best writing buddies to whom you can talk about your writing and your writing life. This is the place to bring your doubts, fears, and insecurities, and admit your flaws and foibles. These are also the people with whom you discuss ideas, work through writing problems (life problems, too). You can even boast some with these friends; they'll applaud your successes and cheer you on. And you'll do the same for them.

- **Writing groups:** This is where you go for critique of your work. To listen to others' ideas, writers whose opinions you trust and whose work you respect. Writing groups meet regularly, monthly at least, often weekly, and are made up of a core group that offers continuity, people who are familiar with your work and you as a writer.

- **Writer's rooms or writer's lofts:** In many cities you can find these places for writing alone, writing together, where people come to do their own work in the company of others. San Diego Writers, Ink, hosts Room to Write; Minneapolis has the Loft; there's the

Office in Santa Monica; Uptown Writer's Space and the Writers WorkSpace in Chicago; the Writers' Room of Boston; and Writers Room in New York. These are just a few we know about. Check the Internet for locations in your area.

- **Classes, workshops, and seminars:** Learn about the craft from writers whose work you admire. Here you'll find teachers and mentors and others who can broaden and deepen your writing world.

- **Conferences:** You learn about the craft at conferences; participants often have the opportunity to meet and interact with editors and agents as well. Shawguides.com is an excellent site to discover writing conferences in the United States and around the world. *Poets & Writers* magazine also lists them, as do other publications, such as *Writer's Digest* and *The Writer* magazine.

- **Readings and book signings:** Here's a chance to hear authors read their own work and to meet and chat with writers you might otherwise never meet.

- **The Internet:** Everything from online chats to Q&As to guest appearances and lectures by authors. Blogs, podcasts, videos, and real-time writing groups and writing gurus. Plus opportunities to publish your work, find agents, take classes, and hook up with writers across the country and around the world. You'll find listings of all things writerly, from events to books on writing, publications, and more. In fact, you can find so much about writing and writers that you can spend hours browsing and linking and getting deeper and deeper inside the web. A hint: get your daily writing in before you see what's up in cyberspace.

> For writing practice to be complete, we must give it away: the effort, the results, and identification with the results.
>
> ⌒ GAIL SHER ⌒

{*See also* Find Your Tribe: Why Hang Out with Other Writers, p. 173; How to Start a Writing Practice Group, p. 223}

IT'S ALL COPY

Writers live life on two levels: one where we participate in relationships, go about our daily business, interact, respond, and perform; the other in which we observe and take notes. We can't help it. It's in our writer's bones. Part and parcel of being a writer.

When Nora Ephron's mother was in the hospital on her deathbed, she told her daughter, "Take notes, it's all copy." Everything we observe, all that we are part of, all our feelings, thoughts, reflections, and prayers, the aggregate of all that happens, goes into the stew pot from which we ladle our work. No need to feel you have nothing to write about; you have everything. "There are significant moments in everyone's day that can make literature," said Raymond Carver. "That's what you ought to write about."

For example, you're writing a play and your character is holding her baby. You remember the time you held your own child against your breast, that she weighed less than a bag of oranges. You pause in your writing, form your arms around a phantom baby, and remember your infant in that warm nest, the faint drumming of her heart against your own. You remember the sweet roundness of her cheek and how her lips bowed together, wet and pink. When you lean down to take in her scent, those long-ago feelings of love and protection rise on the intake of your breath. It is from within this real-life scene stored away in your writer's memory that you resume your writing.

At times it may feel immoral or even exploitive to take such notes, as a scene in Lorrie Moore's award-winning story "People Like That Are the Only People Here" illustrates. The story tells of a couple whose baby is diagnosed with cancer. The husband tells his writer wife, "Take notes. We are going to need the money." "No. I can't," the mother says. "Not this! I write fiction. This isn't fiction." When my own father was dying and I sat beside him on the edge of a cold, vinyl-covered hospital chair, I didn't want to notice his ropy hands wrapped around the aluminum bars of his bed, willed myself to not look at the color of his toenails, blue as a bruise under the awful fluorescent lights. But my experience

> Write about what hurts, what broke your heart. Write about what you don't understand. Write about what you can't forget. Write about your regrets and your outrage.
>
> ⮞ JOHN DUFRESNE ⮜

was like Lorrie Moore's character's, who, at the end of the story, says, "Here are the notes."

So even as you kiss your lover and lean against his naked chest, you make note of the curve of his neck as it gives way to shoulder, the muscles in his back; even as you watch in terror as your three-year-old tumbles from the jungle gym, you observe the way her tiny body free-falls through space and the look of disbelief in her eyes. These are the notes and scratches with which you fill your notebooks, like a squirrel storing for winter, nuts of experience and observation that will feed your writing. Fair warning to such lovers, family, friends, and acquaintances: you're a writer, and it's all grist for your writing mill.

> When what we see catches us off guard, and when we write it as realistically and openly as possible, it offers hope.
>
> ⌒ ANNE LAMOTT ⌒

{*See also* Transferring Real Life to Fiction, p. 201; Writing about Real People, p. 155; Truth versus Fact, p. 114}

WRITING AS THE JOURNEY

We get aboard the soul train of writing not for the destination but for the journey. The journey of self-discovery, of exploring the hinterlands of our imaginations, of finding our voices and telling our stories. To make our own loud noise.

Great though it may be to publish, publishing is not the purpose of writing. In the end, being published will not change your life, but writing will. If you are to be a writer who writes, you will never be finished. Stories may pass beneath your pen, or essays, poems, plays, books, fiction, or nonfiction. Don't worry that you'll run out of ideas or subjects. You won't. Always, always there will be something more to write.

Think of this: No one is more qualified than you to write what you want to write. You're the only one who has ever lived your life. No one else can tell the stories you can tell in the voice you can tell them. "Everyone is talented, original and has something important to say," said Brenda Ueland.

No one else can tell you what to write, either. No editors, or agents, or publishers, or teachers, or friends or lovers. Sometimes not even your thinking, rational mind can tell you where you're going on this writing journey. "Ah, Paris in the spring," it may say, but you find yourself in Fargo in February and a blizzard's blowing in.

> Whereas wealth and fame have a way of not happening, the enhanced self brought to birth through written words always does, owing to this neat reciprocity: Your writing creates you as you create it.
>
> ⬢ REG SANER ⬢

How brave we are to sign on for the journey. To trust the direction we receive from our inner guide and follow the road before us even though we can't see where it's taking us. Can't, in fact, even see around the bend.

But here we are, like Lewis and Clark. Canoes packed. Journals in hand. Setting out for the far and distant shore. Following some inner calling that urges us to leave behind the known and journey to what lies beyond.

Bon voyage.

BEYOND PRACTICE

WRITING RETREATS

To retreat is to withdraw, and for writers this means withdrawing from the daily world to a place where your writer-self is nurtured and cared for. You can retreat at home by closing yourself off from outside disturbances, disconnecting the phone and remaining in solitude, or go elsewhere, to a friend's cabin in the woods, a bed-and-breakfast in the next town, a retreat center across the country.

Retreats can last for half a day, half a month, or half a year. Dian retreats for a twenty-four-hour period of every week, Sandy goes away for one month every year, Roger stayed in Spain for more than a year. For this Beyond Practice writing retreat, include at least one overnight so you can breathe deeply and refill yourself, give time to simply being. Invite one or two writing friends if you like, more if the space allows, or go alone if solitude is more appealing. The idea of retreat is to rest, summon quiet, and replenish.

For the past few years, several writer friends and I have created retreats together. This is how our retreats are structured, more or less: The first day is a time of arriving. Each person brings simple food to share; books and journals; music, perhaps; notebooks; and maybe a manuscript to read aloud. After dinner, we may schedule a brief writing session, just for warming up and setting out intentions. More often than not, we spend the evening allowing our bodies to rest and our souls to transition.

> Never forget: This very moment, we can change our lives. There never was a moment, and never will be, when we are without the power to alter our destiny.
>
> ⌒ STEVEN PRESSFIELD ⌒

Next morning, each awakes as she will; there is no schedule — some will share breakfast; others begin with a walk and journal writing. A writing session begins at nine. Working from words or phrases each offers on tiny slips of paper piled in the center of the table, we do five-, ten-, fifteen-, ten-, and five-minute writes, reading after each. After the morning session, some plan activities together; some go solo. Another writing session is scheduled for half past two, and following that, the afternoon is free until dinner together in the evening. After dinner, someone reads a manuscript. The next day is more of the same, and so on.

Follow this outline, or be even less structured, and let the writing come as it will.

One summer my friend Carol and I borrowed a friend's condominium in Colorado and spent ten days with our novels. We also managed to soak in the hot springs, take a day trip to a nearby town, see some amazing scenery, and eat very well.

> Silence is a writer's familiar. Silence, earned or merely present, is as natural to writers as writing.
>
> ⌒ JAYNE ANNE PHILLIPS ⌒

You may want to bring specific projects to work on when you go on retreat, but also take long walks, gaze out windows, eat leisurely and simply. Leave your watch at home and let your body tell you when to eat, when to sleep, when to move, and when to be still. Light candles, build a fire, watch the rain. Attune yourself to the sensory.

Here are some prompts to take along.

- Write about promises broken
- Write about the last light of day
- Write about a secret collection
- Write what whispers your name in the night
- Notes drawn from the river
- Write about a whole life of madness
- This is where I've been

ACKNOWLEDGMENTS

After nearly twenty years, the roll call of writers with whom I have shared writing practice sessions would fill more than a few pages. Add to that the names of students and participants who've been in my classes and workshops and groups, and the text becomes unwieldy. But if there were space enough, and if my memory would hold up, I would list them all, because each session and each writer has added to the making and remaking of this book. Thank you all, writers and kindred spirits; and thank you, San Diego Writers, Ink, for your warm and generous community.

My appreciation and gratitude go to:

Georgia Hughes, practical, professional, and amazingly patient editor, who said, "Let's do it again." What a pleasure to work with someone who brings common sense and creative ideas together in a way that enhances both, and who makes it all seem so easy. Thank you for giving new life to my first and favorite book.

A thousand blessings to my teacher and friend Janet Fitch for writing the foreword to this edition.

Thanks to Tracy Cunningham for a bold and beautiful cover design, and for relaunching the flying book. To Tona Pearce Myers and Megan Colman, for another inspired interior design and always-detailed attention to the craft of typesetting. And to Kristen Cashman, whose copyediting skills go way beyond knowledge of proper grammar and correct punctuation. I am grateful for your expertise, your meticulous attention to detail and nuance, and the lessons in English usage that I so obviously needed.

Appreciation goes to Jonathan Wichmann, publicist Kim Corbin, and the rest of the professional staff at New World Library. I am honored to have this decade-long association with a publishing house whose books bring so much beauty to the world. Thank you, Munro Magruder and Marc Allen.

I would be remiss if I didn't acknowledge the talented and generous people who were instrumental in the first edition of this book. My thanks go to Gina Misiroglu, editor of the original edition; Mary Ann Casler, who designed the cover and made the flying book an icon; and Doris Doi, my colleague of many years whose talent and creativity were invaluable in the original concept.

Thank you, members of Thursday Writers and Brown Bag groups who completed the writing practice questionnaire. The notes on your experience were illuminating and helpful.

Family and friends, foremost and always: how patient and loving and supportive you are and have always been. And did I say patient? I love you, son and daughter-in-law, Chris and Stephanie, and who has more beautiful, talented grandchildren than mine, Andrew and Alexandra? Amy, whatever I did right to get you for a daughter, I am both amazed and grateful. Jackie, your commitment to your art and craft inspires me, and Craig, you're pretty darned inspirational, too. Sister writers and dearheart friends, Dian Greenwood and Drusilla Campbell, you are models for how to do and keep doing it and looking so good while you do it. Thank you, Dawn Rowland, for asking the right questions and for cheering me on. Camille Soleil, you are the *soleil* of my life. Thank you, Roger Aplon, for your steadfastness and generous heart and for your poetry.

I am especially grateful to Steve Montgomery, my Thursday Writers cohort and beloved friend whose support and cohortism have made all the difference.

RECOMMENDED READING

I'll admit it. I like books. I like to hold them and smell them and take them to bed with me. I like to prop them up while I eat lunch and pack them in my suitcase when I travel. Don't get me wrong — I like the Internet, too. I have some favorite writing sites and bloggers, and like others I know, I spend way too much time online, browsing and linking and downloading. But when it comes to recommended reading, I'm going to stay with my first love: books. Here are just a few, mostly about writing in general — the attitude and philosophy of writing, inspirational rather than instructional — though there are a few that lay out writing exercises. There are, of course, many, many more books on writing. Creating this short list was like choosing an ice cream at Ben & Jerry's, an exercise filled with indecision followed by regret for what I didn't select.

Ackerman, Diane. *A Natural History of the Senses*. New York: Random House, 1990.

Aronie, Nancy Slonim. *Writing from the Heart: Tapping the Power of Your Inner Voice*. New York: Hyperion, 1998.

Baldwin, Christina. *Storycatcher: Making Sense of Our Lives through the Power and Practice of Story*. Novato, CA: New World Library, 2005.

Bell, Susan. *The Artful Edit: On the Practice of Editing Yourself*. New York: W. W. Norton, 2007.

Bennett, Hal Zina. *Write Starts: Prompts, Quotes, and Exercises to Jumpstart Your Creativity*. Novato, CA: New World Library, 2010.

Bernays, Anne, and Pamela Painter. *What If?: Writing Exercises for Fiction Writers*. Second edition. New York: Pearson Longman, 2004.

Bradbury, Ray. *Zen in the Art of Writing: Essays on Creativity*. Santa Barbara, CA: Joshua Odell Editions, 1994.

Burroway, Janet. *Writing Fiction: A Guide to Narrative Craft*. Eighth edition. New York: Longman, 2010.

Butler, Robert Olen. *From Where You Dream: The Process of Writing Fiction*. New York: Grove, 2005.

Cameron, Julia. *The Artist's Way: A Spiritual Path to Higher Creativity*. Los Angeles: Jeremy Tarcher, 1992.

Dillard, Annie. *The Writing Life*. New York: Harper & Row, 1989.

Dufresne, John. *The Lie That Tells a Truth: A Guide to Writing Fiction*. New York: Norton, 2003.

Ellis, Sherry, ed. *Now Write!: Fiction Writing Exercises from Today's Best Writers and Teachers*. New York: Jeremy Tarcher/Penguin, 2006.

Goldberg, Natalie. *Wild Mind: Living the Writer's Life*. New York: Bantam, 1990.

———. *Writing Down the Bones: Freeing the Writer Within*. Boston/London: Shambhala, 1986.

Johnston, Bret Anthony, ed. *Naming the World: And Other Exercises for the Creative Writer*. New York: Random House, 2007.

King, Stephen. *On Writing: A Memoir of the Craft*. New York: Scribner, 2000.

Lamott, Anne. *Bird by Bird: Some Instructions on Writing and Life*. New York: Pantheon, 1994.

Lerner, Betsy. *The Forest for the Trees: An Editor's Advice to Writers*. New York: Riverhead Books/Penguin Putnam, 2000.

Maisel, Eric. *Deep Writing: 7 Principles that Bring Ideas to Life*. New York: Jeremy Tarcher/Putnam, 1999.

———. *Fearless Creating: A Step-by-Step Guide to Starting and Completing Your Work of Art*. New York: Jeremy Tarcher/Putnam, 1995.

Nachmanovitch, Stephen. *Free Play: The Power of Improvisation in Life and the Arts*. New York: Jeremy Tarcher/Putnam, 1990.

Prose, Francine. *Reading Like a Writer: A Guide for People Who Love Books and for Those Who Want to Write Them*. New York: HarperCollins, 2006.

Schneider, Pat. *The Writer as an Artist: A New Approach to Writing Alone and with Others*. Los Angeles: Lowell House, 1993.

See, Carolyn. *Making a Literary Life: Advice for Writers and Other Dreamers*. New York: Ballantine, 2002.

Sher, Gail. *One Continuous Mistake: Four Noble Truths for Writers*. New York: Penguin/Putnam, 1999.

Thomas, Abigail. *Thinking about Memoir*. New York: AARP/Sterling, 2008.

Ueland, Brenda. *If You Want to Write: A Book about Art, Independence and Spirit*. St. Paul, MN: Gray Wolf Press, 1987.

Wooldridge, Susan G. *Poemcrazy: Freeing Your Life with Words*. New York: Clarkson Potter, 1996.

ABOUT THE AUTHOR

Judy Reeves is a writer, teacher, and writing practice provocateur who has written four books on writing. Her work has appeared in magazines, journals, and anthologies and on the spoken word compilation *First Friday: Year 3*. She has edited several books and chapbooks, including *Brown Bag Anthology*, a collection of writings from the first five years of her writing practice groups at The Writing Center, a nonprofit literary arts organization, which she cofounded.

In addition to leading writing practice groups, which she has done for over seventeen years, Judy holds private workshops, teaches at University of California San Diego Extension; San Diego Writers, Ink; and writing conferences internationally. She is a regular speaker at the Southern California Writers Conferences, where she is especially known for her lively, late-night Rogues read-and-critique workshops. In 2004, she cofounded San Diego Writers, Ink, with a committed group of volunteers, and served as its executive director.

Born in the Midwest, Judy has traveled throughout the world. She is forever grateful to her father for bringing their family to San Diego, where she currently lives.

WWW. JUDYREEVESWRITER.COM

NEW WORLD LIBRARY is dedicated to publishing books and other media that inspire and challenge us to improve the quality of our lives and the world.

We are a socially and environmentally aware company, and we strive to embody the ideals presented in our publications. We recognize that we have an ethical responsibility to our customers, our staff members, and our planet.

We serve our customers by creating the finest publications possible on personal growth, creativity, spirituality, wellness, and other areas of emerging importance. We serve New World Library employees with generous benefits, significant profit sharing, and constant encouragement to pursue their most expansive dreams.

As a member of the Green Press Initiative, we print an increasing number of books with soy-based ink on 100 percent postconsumer-waste recycled paper. Also, we power our offices with solar energy and contribute to nonprofit organizations working to make the world a better place for us all.

Our products are available
in bookstores everywhere.
For our catalog, please contact:

New World Library
14 Pamaron Way
Novato, California 94949

Phone: 415-884-2100 or 800-972-6657
Catalog requests: Ext. 50
Orders: Ext. 52
Fax: 415-884-2199
Email: escort@newworldlibrary.com

To subscribe to our electronic newsletter, visit
www.newworldlibrary.com

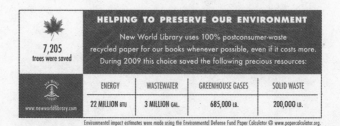

HELPING TO PRESERVE OUR ENVIRONMENT

7,205 trees were saved

New World Library uses 100% postconsumer-waste recycled paper for our books whenever possible, even if it costs more. During 2009 this choice saved the following precious resources:

ENERGY	WASTEWATER	GREENHOUSE GASES	SOLID WASTE
22 MILLION BTU	3 MILLION GAL.	685,000 LB.	200,000 LB.

www.newworldlibrary.com

Environmental impact estimates were made using the Environmental Defense Fund Paper Calculator @ www.papercalculator.org.